CONTENTS

CONQUERING YOUR OWN
GOLIATHS

Then said David to the Philistine, Thou comest to me with a sword, and with a spear, and with a shield: But I come to thee in the name of the Lord of hosts, the God of the armies of Israel, whom thou hast defied.

This day will the Lord deliver thee into mine hand . . . that all the earth may know that there is a God in Israel.

And all this assembly shall know that the Lord saveth not with sword and spear: for the battle is the Lord's, and he will give you into our hands.

1 Samuel 17:45-47

Steven A. Cramer

Deseret Book Company
Salt Lake City, Utah

To my wife, LoAnne,
whose editing helped this book
become what I wanted it to be.

Library of Congress Cataloging-in-Publication Data

Cramer, Steven A.
    Conquering your own Goliaths / by Steven A. Cramer.
      p.   cm.
    Includes index.
    ISBN 0-87579-156-5
    1. Christian life—Mormon authors. I. Title.
BX8656.C73   1988
248.4'89332—dc19   88-25669
                                      CIP

Printed in the United States of America

10   9   8   7   6   5   4

PREFACE

When our youngest daughter, Kristy, was about a year and a half old, she suffered a serious illness for several weeks. In an attempt to determine the cause, the doctors decided to make some extensive blood tests.

I took Kristy to the lab where the nurse was to draw her blood. I knew she would cry when the nurse pricked her little finger, but I consoled myself with its necessity, expecting it would soon be over. However, I was not at all prepared for what was about to take place. Because Kristy's fingers were so tiny, the nurse had trouble getting enough blood. She squeezed and squeezed her finger. Poor little Kristy was so frightened that I had to use all my strength to keep her hand still and to keep her from wrenching free.

After what seemed like an hour, the nurse finally squeezed enough blood from her tiny finger to fill the capillary tube, and laid it aside. At last this is over, I thought, but before I could even begin to comfort Kristy, the nurse pricked a second finger and began to fill another tube. Kristy's fear and screaming increased, and no words can describe the heart-wrenching agony I suffered as that determined nurse worked her way through all five fingers on Kristy's poor little hand, and then went on to the next until she had inflicted all ten fingers.

How I struggled, trying not to hate the nurse. I wanted to jump out of the chair with my little girl and run to safety where I could hold her tight and assure her of my love.

Those few minutes seemed to take a lifetime, and I wondered if Kristy would ever trust me again. I wished I could help her understand why all this was necessary. I knew her suffering was required for the doctors to learn the cause of her illness, but how could an eighteen-month-old baby understand that?

The worst part of this experience was the bewildered and tortured look of accusation I saw in Kristy's eyes, as though she was pleading and asking through her pain and fright: "Daddy, how can you allow this? I thought you loved me. Why are you doing this to me?"

I would have given anything to have taken her place and spared her from that suffering, but there was no way I could substitute for her. She alone could pay the price for her healing.

Our Savior felt that same kind of love and compassion, only magnified a million times, for our pain, for the penalty we each would be required to pay throughout eternity if he had not come to rescue us.

While I could not pay the price for Kristy, Jesus Christ could pay our debt, and he did pay it. But all his suffering and sacrifice is worthless in our day-to-day lives until we learn to appreciate and put it first in our lives.

In this book we will discuss how to take advantage of his atonement, how to overcome unresolved guilt and other spiritual barriers that keep us apart from God, and how to conquer the Goliath-sized weaknesses and habits that prevent us from enjoying the fullness of his love.

RESCUE

The story is told of a ship that was struggling through the icy waters of the north during a great storm one night. As the ship was tossed violently from wave to wave and the heavy seas crashed down upon the deck, one of the sailors raced to the bridge, shouting, "Captain, Captain, stop the ship. Man overboard!"

The captain paused only a split second and then replied, "No, there is no way we could control the ship if we were to stop the engines. In this turbulence it would be suicide to put men into a rowboat for a search. And even if they could stay afloat in this rough sea, the man would be drowned in the icy waters long before we could ever locate him in the dark. I'm sorry, but the man is lost. There is no way to save him."

"But Captain," the seaman protested, "it's your own son!"

Needless to say, the captain stopped the ship and took every risk possible to rescue his son.

Every child of God is a "man overboard" with some kind of sin or bad habit as he or she drifts and drowns in the storms of evil that fill this wicked world. Our Savior took the greatest risk of all at Gethsemane and Calvary to rescue us from eternal damnation and lead us joyfully back to our Heavenly Father.

When we think of all Jesus did during his ministry, we sometimes lose sight of the fact that the primary reason he came to this earth was to rescue us from Satan's power. In Luke 19:10 the Savior said that "the Son of man is come to seek and to save that which was lost." In 1 Timothy 1:15 we

1

read, "This is a faithful saying, and worthy of all acceptation, that Christ Jesus came into the world to save sinners." There should be no shame in the fact that we all need him, for without our Savior's help, we would all be lost.

The Jews did not recognize Christ as the long-awaited Messiah because they were looking for a militant leader who would free them from Roman oppression. But Jesus came to rescue them from an even greater captivity: the self-imposed slavery of hate, resentment, bitterness, self-condemnation, unresolved guilt, weaknesses, bad habits, even addictions.

Jesus had a unique opportunity to explain this in the Nazareth synagogue when they gave him the place of honor to read from the scriptures and then offer the commentary. Of all the Old Testament prophecies of his coming, the one he chose to best describe the purpose of his holy mission was a verse from Isaiah: "He hath sent me to heal the brokenhearted, to preach deliverance to the captives, and recovering of sight to the blind, to set at liberty them that are bruised." (Luke 4:18; compare Isa. 61:1.)

Significantly, the verse he chose did not speak of the resurrection, as important as that is. There was no pronouncement of his power or glory, no threat to the Roman conquerors, not even a criticism of the apostate and misguided rabbis and priests. Instead, he chose a verse that emphasized his love, compassion, and understanding for our broken hearts and our mental and emotional hurts and bruises. He said he came to give us the power and the truth to restore our spiritual vision that we might see the way out of our difficulties. He came to rescue us from the captivity of enslaving habits. He came with the mission to release us, through the power of his love and forgiveness, into a life of abundance and joy.

Jesus came to help those whom the world labels as losers: the failures, the sinners, the rejects and outcasts. He came to help people who are hurting, people who are confused and discouraged, people who have made mistakes but want to get right with themselves and with God. His gospel is not given for perfect people, but for sinners.

His greatest desire is not for fame or position, but to wrap us in the arms of his love and remove every obstacle that prevents us from being all Heavenly Father means us to be. How great is his desire to convince each of us that we are important and precious to him. A favorite hymn describes God's love for us:

> Come unto Jesus, ye heavy laden,
> Careworn and fainting, by sin oppressed.
> He'll safely guide you unto that haven
> Where all who trust him may rest.
>
> Come unto Jesus; He'll ever heed you,
> Though in the darkness you've gone astray.
> His love will find you and gently lead you
> From darkest night into day.
> (*Hymns*, 1985, no. 117.)

Big Ben was in prison for molesting children. He hated himself for what he had done, and he thought everyone else must hate him too, especially the Lord. Because he didn't understand the infinite power of the Savior to cleanse our past, even from something as wicked as he had done, Big Ben felt lost and hopeless.

I'm glad he gave me permission to share his story, because many of us are also in prison but don't realize it. We are imprisoned by unconquered weaknesses and sins, by the iron bars of unresolved guilt and self-condemnation. Like Big Ben, many are held captive by Satan's lie that we have "gone too far" and that God could not possibly love us after the mistakes we have made.

For two years Big Ben lived in bitter isolation, rejecting all efforts of the LDS chaplain and others to love him and help him find the way back. When the time finally came that he was ready to pray, he hid in a janitor's closet so no one would see him. He said: "I fell to my knees on the concrete floor and opened my heart to the Christ. I wept and begged him to forgive me for what I had been doing. I pleaded to be acceptable and to find the path back to him.

"As I talked with him, I felt the terrible burden I had been carrying for so long gently lifted from my shoulders. I felt a warm comforting spirit around me. It was so strong that I felt I could have reached out and touched my Lord.

"I was allowed to know that I had never been alone here, that even Christ had been called names as I had, that I was forgiven and loved by him and that I could yet be counted a member of his Church and attain heights greater than I could imagine."

Eventually I was privileged to visit Big Ben there in prison, and we embraced. As his big old arms reached around me and pressed me close to him, I thanked the Lord for the love of God that rescues and changes every person who allows it to come into his life. God loves us exactly as we are right now, but he loves us too much to leave us that way. He does not demand that we change *before* he loves us, because he knows that if we need changing, discovering the reality of his love *will* change us.

Big Ben's experience demonstrates that God does not condemn the *sinner,* but only the *sin,* and this knowledge should give us confidence in approaching him.

One of the great themes of the scriptures is that no one can fall below the reach of God's infinite, unconditional, and unwavering love. There is absolutely nothing that a person can do to make God love him more than he already does, and there is nothing one can do that will cause God to love him any less.

In New Testament times, nothing was considered as repulsive and abhorrent as the leper. Everywhere he went, the leper was required to warn people by calling out, "Unclean, unclean, stand clear." And that is exactly how Satan wants us to feel when we sin: "Unclean, unclean, stand clear. Don't love me, don't respect me, don't get involved in my life — unclean."

But Jesus was not repulsed by the lepers. Without hesitation he said the same thing to them that he says to each of us: "Come to me." And when they came, he actually reached out and touched them! That fearless touch of love and acceptance amazed the Jews far more than the healing did.

Though we are all spiritual lepers, there is no sin great enough, no filthiness repulsive enough to separate us from the healing touch of our Savior's love if we will only open our hearts and accept it. He says: "Behold, I stand at the door, and knock: if *any* man hear my voice, and open the door, I will come in to him." (Rev. 3:20; emphasis added.)

CONQUERING YOUR OWN GOLIATHS

The story of David and Goliath can help us overcome our own problems — problems that often seem as large as a Goliath. You will recall that there was a war between Israel and the Philistines. The two armies were camped on opposing mountainsides with a steep valley or ravine between them. Across this narrow valley the two armies could see and hear each other.

Each day the Philistines sent Goliath out to challenge Israel to provide their champion. The plan was for these two men to fight and thereby determine the victor without the necessity of the two armies fighting. David was too young to be in the army; but his three elder brothers were there, and his father sent David to take supplies to them and see how they were.

Shortly after David arrived at the camp, Goliath roared his challenge across the valley: "Am not I a Philistine, and ye servants to Saul? Choose you a man for you, and let him come down to me." (1 Sam. 17:8.)

How surprised David must have been when he saw the reaction of Israel's soldiers. Even though they were safely separated by the ravine, and even though they had heard this same challenge for forty days in a row, they were still so afraid that they literally ran from the camp. (1 Sam. 17:16, 24.)

They had good reason to fear. Goliath was nearly ten feet

tall. His legs, arms, and even his neck were protected by brass armor. He wore a brass helmet and carried an enormous shield. He was so big that his armor weighed over 150 pounds. His spear was so huge that the metal tip alone weighed over 18 pounds. No wonder they were afraid!

We all have our own personal Goliaths to face, giant Goliaths of opposition, adversity, and temptation that we cannot conquer without the help of God. Some of us, for example, are overcome by the Goliaths of drugs, alcohol, overeating, and other compulsive addictions or enslaving habits. Some of us face the Goliaths of financial problems like unemployment or debt. Many must fight the giants of evil thoughts and immorality.

Others find their Goliath right in their own marriage, which may be threatened by infidelity, sarcasm, hurts and criticisms, and even by the indifference of love they have allowed to grow cold. And while these people are desecrating their sacred marriage covenants, many singles face the Goliath of loneliness.

Almost everyone faces the emotional Goliaths of discouragement, depression, and feelings of inferiority.

Satan loves all these Goliaths. He wants us to believe that they are too big for us to conquer, that we are inferior and incapable of attaining the celestial kingdom.

The wonderful message of the story of David and Goliath is that it is not necessary to live lives filled with fear, misery, and defeat. Jesus Christ came to give us victory over our own Goliaths, and it is a terrible tragedy when we settle for anything less than total victory, because it is so unnecessary.

I think what really got David's attention was the final insult that Goliath hurled across the valley: "I defy the armies of Israel. . . . Give me a man that we may fight together." (1 Sam. 17:10.) That insult was more than David could take. Looking at the quaking soldiers, he angrily demanded, "Who is this uncircumcised Philistine, that he should defy the armies of the living God?" (1 Sam. 17:26.)

How could it be that the trained, experienced, and armed

soldiers of Israel quaked in fear, while David, who was but a lad, and unexperienced in the ways of war, was not afraid to engage this giant in combat? Perhaps the soldiers were afraid of Goliath for the same reason we fear our own Goliaths — they viewed his challenge in terms of their own limited strength and abilities. They did not understand the grace that makes it possible for God to give us strength and ability beyond our natural limitations.

But David knew something they did not. He knew that when we are partners with the Lord, the power to overcome our problems is not restricted to the limitations of our own mortal abilities. With Ammon, in the Book of Mormon, David could easily have told them, "I know that I am nothing; as to my strength I am weak; therefore I will not boast of myself, but I will boast of my God, *for in his strength, I can do all things.*" (Alma 26:12; emphasis added. See also Philip. 4:13.) Notice the valiant words David said to Goliath: "Thou comest to me with a sword, and with a spear, and with a shield: But I come to thee in the name of the Lord of hosts, the God of the armies of Israel, whom thou hast defied. This day will the Lord deliver thee into mine hand . . . and all this assembly shall know that the Lord saveth not with sword and spear, *for the battle is the Lord's* and he will give you into our hands." (1 Sam. 17:45-47; emphasis added.)

In the Latter-day Saint edition of the King James Bible, these inspiring words of David are cross-referenced to D&C 105:14, where the Lord Jesus Christ promised, "As I said in a former commandment, even so will I fulfill. . . . *I will fight your battles.*" (Emphasis added.)

This is important doctrine. The Lord has repeated it many times. Consider these verses: "Inasmuch as ye are humble and faithful and call upon my name, behold, *I will give you the victory.*" (D&C 104:82; emphasis added.)

"For the Lord your God is he that goeth with you, to fight for you against your enemies, to save you." (Deut. 20:4.)

"And Christ hath said: *If ye will have faith in me ye shall have power* to do whatsoever thing is expedient in me." (Moro. 7:33; emphasis added.)

Something profound happens when we personalize the scriptures by inserting our own name into them, as if God had spoken them to us personally, which, in effect, he has. ("What I say unto *one* I say unto *all.*" [D&C 82:5.])

I experienced incredible joy and relief when I put my name in those scriptures and discovered that God didn't expect me to do it all by myself. For example:

"Steven, as I said in a former commandment, even so will I fulfill, I will fight your battles."

"Christ hath said to me, Steven, if ye will have faith in me ye shall have power to do whatsoever thing is expedient in me."

Let us go back to Goliath. David boldly went down the ravine, stopped at the brook to gather five smooth stones, put one of them into his sling, and hurled that stone with deadly force and accuracy deep into Goliath's forehead. Using Goliath's own sword, David cut off his head and created an eternal symbol for the destruction of every person's Goliaths.

This story is not in the scriptures just for historical knowledge. It is there to guide us in the way we respond to our own Goliaths. No longer need we fear when we find ourselves with our back to the wall, facing a mental, emotional, or spiritual giant that towers above our own limited resources. Now we can meet them confidently and courageously, knowing that our Savior will be there to help fight the battle and assure the victory.

In D&C 50:35 we are promised that no worthy member of the Church need suffer enslavement to any Goliath because "the kingdom is given you of the Father, *and power to overcome all things which are not ordained of him.*" (Emphasis added.) In the January 1981 *New Era,* Lloyd Poelman cited an example of this. He met his Goliath at a temporary job with a construction company. Unemployment was high, jobs were scarce, and this job was paying more than Lloyd had ever earned before.

He really wanted to make good, especially since his mission was only three months away.

His Goliath was ninety-six feet long and weighed several tons. It was a steel parking barrier that had been pulled from the ground by a huge crane. Like a giant comb lying on the ground, the steel guard rail was welded to thirteen posts, which were each embedded in huge gobs of concrete. Lloyd's assignment was to break the concrete loose from each of the thirteen posts so that they could be dismantled and carried away.

The boss gave him a sledgehammer and stood to watch. Eager to prove himself, Lloyd raised the hammer and hit the first mass of concrete with all his strength.

Nothing happened.

He hit it several times in the same spot, but hardly a chip broke loose. Acutely aware of the boss's stare, Lloyd feared that if he didn't show some quick progress in breaking the cement, he would soon be out of a job. He continued to hammer away with no success. As the boss walked away in disgust, Lloyd prayed.

He told the Lord that he knew this job was an answer to prayer, but he would need divine assistance if he was going to keep it. He reminded the Lord that the money wasn't for something selfish, like a yellow convertible, but for his mission.

Describing his prayer, Lloyd said, "I didn't expect him to send a host of angels with sledgehammers, but I knew that somehow he could help me." I like that. We don't have to know how God is going to meet our needs before we can exercise faith. We only need to trust that he will come to our aid as he has promised. As the Apostle Paul wrote: "My God shall supply all your need according to his riches in glory by Christ Jesus." (Philip. 4:19.)

Lloyd received an immediate answer to his prayer: "Strike the steel." He didn't understand why he should hit the steel, but he obeyed.

As large chunks of cement began cracking apart, he realized that the blows on the steel were sending a series of strong vibrations through the center of the cement. After only two hours of work, the entire steel railing was free of the concrete, which Lloyd had neatly stacked in piles.

Imagine his excitement as he jubilantly walked over to the boss, with his sledgehammer slung casually on his shoulder, and said, "I'll need some help moving the railing out of the driveway."

Assuming that Lloyd had given up, the boss angrily led the way back to the parking lot. When he rounded the corner, he stopped dead in his tracks. His jaw dropped and he stood silent for a long time. Then he said, "Lloyd, you're welcome to stay on this job as long as you like." Lloyd worked there the next three months, earning an excellent wage.

You may feel defeated by your Goliaths. You may feel overwhelmed by habits and weaknesses that seem insurmountable, as if they were embedded in concrete. But God knows how *each person* can "strike the steel," and if you will allow it, he will not only teach you how but will also give you the strength to do it, just as he did for David, just as he did for me.

As a young boy I fell captive to the Goliath of masturbation. Eventually, I also became addicted to pornography, and these two giant Goliath-habits held me captive to my carnal nature for the next twenty years. My addiction to pornography was so strong that every time I felt lonely or discouraged, or even if I merely walked by a magazine display, I would be seized with an overwhelming compulsion to indulge in that vile trash.

I tried not to give in to these temptations. I tried hard. But often, when seized by such attacks, I lost control and went on pornographic binges, much like an alcoholic who goes back to drink after a period of abstinence. Sometimes I spent hundreds of dollars a week on magazines and adult movies.

But eventually, I'd become so saturated in the filth that I would hate myself for what I was doing, and that self-disgust and guilt would give me the strength to throw it all away and begin the process of repentance again. Part of me was determined to conquer this Goliath and live worthy of the celestial kingdom, but deep inside there was another part of me that was equally determined to continue in the sin.

Sometimes, by exercising supreme willpower, I could with- hold myself from the sin for several months at a time, and this was wonderful. But even during those periods of abstinence, the other part of me, the rotten part that loved the sin, would be growing stronger and more insistent. The pressure to give in was like water building up behind a faulty dam, and I became a living Doctor Jekyll and Mr. Hyde in my cycles of indulgence and repentance.

I felt desperate because of this roller-coaster ride. What a horrible way to live. And it is so unnecessary, if we will only accept the power of Christ and allow him to change our carnal natures. But I didn't know that yet, so I struggled for twenty years with this double life, using every tool I could think of to overcome it.

I fasted and prayed. I attended my meetings and served in the Church. I studied scriptures for several hours a day. I read dozens of psychology, motivational, and self-improvement books. I set goals. I made promises to the Lord. I used positive affirmations. And still I continued to fall back into the filthiness over and over again.

Through all those years of addiction, each fall destroyed part of my self-respect. Each fall made it harder to believe that I would ever be able to repent and finally conquer myself.

Eventually, all those years of lust and compromise led me from the mental adultery to the physical act, and I was excom- municated.

And how could it have been otherwise? We always become and do what we think about the most. No thought is too small to have its effect. If we think it long enough, we are probably going to do it, because the thoughts we hold in our desires and focus of attention are the very blueprints of our future reality. We always reap in our physical life what we have been sowing in our mental life.

For the next two years, in spite of all my willpower and attempts to stop, I continued to suffer that on-again-off-again battle with sin. Instead of improving, I sank deeper into sin and despair.

Through the buffetings that followed my excommunication, I learned what a horror it is to mock God and trample upon sacred covenants. I learned what it is to experience the fury of hell, and to be held captive by a Goliath that only laughed at my puny efforts to resist with nothing but my own willpower.

I know what it is to be in a hole so deep that you can't see a way out. I know what it is to hurt so much, to feel so worthless and hopeless and filthy, to hate yourself for the things you've done and can't stop doing, that you just want to die. No, it's not death you want, but total annihilation—to simply cease to exist. Worse than being excommunicated is feeling so filthy that you dare not even raise your prayers to heaven for forgiveness and help. Worse than being separated from the Church is to be separated from God, with no hope of ever coming back.

When I was excommunicated I thought, "Now I'm really on the edge of the cliff. Now it's do or die. Now I have to control my compulsions or I'll never get back into the Church." I thought being excommunicated would *force* me to control my evil habits. But the gospel doesn't work by force. Going to the celestial kingdom is not based upon suppressing our evil desires with superhuman restraint and willpower, for then the evil is only caged and locked inside us like a ticking time bomb, just waiting for the right temptation to light the fuse.

What is required is a complete transformation of the heart, desires, and fallen human nature. And nothing but the blood, atonement, and grace of Jesus Christ can do that. I did not understand the difference between merely *controlling* a bad habit and allowing Christ to change my heart and nature so that I no longer *wanted* the habit.

The testimony I once heard an atheist give about his conversion to the gospel demonstrates what I mean. After a lifetime of addiction, he could not give up his cigarettes. He wanted to quit. He tried desperately. But he just could not break their hold on him. A friend asked what the problem was.

"Are you praying about it?"

"Of course I'm praying. I'm doing everything I can."

"Well, then there is something wrong here. Tell me what you say in your prayers."

"I say, Heavenly Father, please help me to stop smoking. What else would you say?"

Many of us make the mistake of praying about the *symptoms* instead of the *cause* of our problems. We say: Please help me stop lusting. Please help me stop eating too much. Help me stop yelling at the wife and kids. Please help me stop drinking, or smoking, or taking drugs—or whatever we think our problem is. But these are only *symptoms* of our fallen, carnal nature. And as long as we focus on the symptoms, we forget the cause and lose sight of the solution, the grace of Jesus Christ. The friend said to the former atheist: "No wonder you can't stop smoking. Your prayer is all wrong. All you're asking is for God to help you *control* an evil habit. You should pray: 'Heavenly Father, I *want* to obey this commandment. I *choose* to obey this commandment. Please change my heart. Please remove this evil desire from me so that I *can* obey.' " What a powerful difference!

Jesus Christ is in the business of saving sinners. But he did not come to save us *in* our sins, which is right where we are if we are merely controlling them with willpower. Jesus came to save us *from* our sins, to give us freedom from our *sinfulness.*

Trying to alter deep-seated Goliath habits with willpower and human behavioral techniques alone is about as effective as shooting at a battleship with a BB gun.

No one can change the carnal nature of the heart and disposition by "iron-jawed willpower," or by behavioral techniques and self-improvement programs alone. We may do much good in controlling our behavior, but until we allow Jesus Christ to alter our hearts and desires, we will suffer a continual struggle between the desires of the flesh and the will of the spirit.

The 1969-70 Gospel Doctrine manual emphasized the importance of recognizing our dependence upon Christ to help in the fight against our Goliaths: "Only in him can any man find the strength, the power and the ability to live a godly life. Only in Christ is there power to transform the human mind and the human heart." (*In His Footsteps Today* [Salt Lake City: Deseret Sunday School Union, 1969], p. 4.)

Now please don't misunderstand me. I'm not saying it is wrong to use willpower to restrain our evil habits and desires. Our covenants and commitments, our goals and resolves, our willpower, all that we can do is necessary, but it is insufficient to save us without the transforming power of the Savior.

It is not wrong to read self-help books or to seek the assistance of professional therapists and counselors unless they become substitutes for the Savior, as they did in my case. Let's use all the psychology and human wisdom that we can, but let's not put that at the center of our faith, in place of Christ.

"Your faith should not stand in the wisdom of men, but in the power of God." (1 Cor. 2:5.)

"It is better to trust in the Lord than to put confidence in man." (Ps. 118:8.)

"Only Jesus Christ is uniquely qualified to provide that hope, that confidence, and that strength to overcome the world and rise above our human failings." ("Jesus Christ: Our Savior and Redeemer," Ezra Taft Benson, *Ensign,* November 1983, p. 6.)

It is imperative to recognize that *no one* can ever do enough, by his or her efforts alone, to live the obedient life that will result in exaltation.

But I understood none of this then, so by the time I had been excommunicated two years, I had been pulled back into my sin so many times that I had lost all hope of ever escaping. My spiritual reserves were completely gone. I was so full of hate for the evil creature I had become that I could no longer live with myself. I began planning my suicide.

Before taking my life, I went for a walk along a river, to offer one last prayer of desperation. I told the Lord that I just couldn't go on. I told him that unless he reached out to save me, I would be lost forever, because I just couldn't do it by myself.

I knew that I was unworthy of his help, yet I begged for mercy. Oh, those were bitter words. I felt humiliated for admitting my helplessness. I hated myself for speaking those desperate words of surrender. It seemed to me like the final, overwhelming failure. I felt ashamed, as if this was the lowest I had ever sunk, to beg God for help that I didn't deserve and couldn't earn.

I thought I was at the end when, in reality, I had at last reached the turning point. For it is only in discovering and admitting our need for God's help that our proud and stubborn heart is at last broken, and we throw open the door to receive his healing influence.

Since my rebaptism I have counseled with many people who are working their way out of serious transgressions. One of the pivotal points of change in every situation has been the admission, the gut-level, honest recognition and confession of their utter inability to solve their own problems without the help of a higher power. How often Jesus stressed that we must come unto him, not in the pride of our self-sufficiency, but as a little child who knows he needs help.

"Many people's lives are choked with pride. They are a law unto themselves. They are arrogant. Like wild stallions they bow to no higher authority. They are self-sufficient. Unless they change and come to the Lord with a broken heart and a contrite spirit, they are unable to make spiritual progress.

"The acknowledgment of God as a higher authority and the subjugation of oneself in a humble, prayerful and sweet attitude is the first step one must take to prepare himself for spiritual growth." (*In His Footsteps Today*, p. 286.)

Once I surrendered my life to the Lord, once I acknowledged my need for him, once I allowed him to take control of my life, once I asked for the Father's mercy to apply the blood of Christ to my sins, the Lord literally changed my heart and my nature.

He took away that horrible enslaving love of carnal plea-
sure. He freed me from my lustful compulsions and addictions,
and in their place he blessed me with an overwhelming aware-
ness of his love. Am I still tempted? Of course. But now I am
free. Now I have a choice. Through Jesus Christ, my Goliath
has been slain.

CHRIST IS
"THE WAY"

Every problem we face in overcoming our Goliaths can be traced directly to the weakness in our relationship with the Savior. As Elder Vaughn J. Featherstone has said: "Number one on our agenda, above all else, is faith in Christ. I don't know anything that will take the place of it. *Whenever we find problems in the Church, we usually find them under one of two umbrellas or canopies, either transgression or lack of faith in Christ.*" (*BYU Devotional Speeches of the Year* [Provo, Utah: Brigham Young University Press, 1982-83], p. 145; emphasis added.)

As I struggled to find my way out of the darkness of my excommunication and sin, I was given a dream that helped me discard the substitutes I was using and place my faith where it belonged. I dreamed that I was hiking in the mountains, and I came to a deep ravine that blocked my path. On the other side, Heavenly Father stood with his arms beckoning me to come to him. I immediately decided to build a bridge so that I could cross the gulf and be with him. For days I gathered materials. At last, when all was ready, I retired to my camp, eager to begin construction the next day.

But when I returned to the ravine, I was astonished to discover that someone had already placed a bridge across the gulf. I couldn't believe it had been done so quickly. It seemed impossible. Who had done this great work for me?

I awoke, pondering the meaning of my dream. It was made known to me that the gulf, or ravine, symbolized the barriers of guilt and self-condemnation I was clinging to, even though I had long since abandoned my evil ways. By trying to punish myself and pay for my sins with self-deprecation, I had created barriers that were preventing me from receiving God's love and forgiveness.

It was also made known to me that it was not necessary to design and build my own bridge to cross that gulf and return to Heavenly Father, because that bridge had already been provided through the love and atonement of Jesus Christ. He is the Bridge.

I was reminded of the Savior's declaration in John 14:6: "I am the way." I was told that it is foolish and self-defeating to try to find our way back to the Father by any means other than the atonement, for hadn't the Savior declared emphatically that "no man cometh unto the Father but by me." (John 14:6.) I also remembered having read the following quotation: "We think we must climb to a certain height of goodness before we can reach God. But He says not 'at the end of the way you may find me;' He says, 'I am the way; I am the road under your feet, the road that begins just as low down as you happen to be.'

"If we are in a hole then The Way begins in the hole. The moment we set our face in the same direction as His, we are walking with God." (Quoted by William R. Parker & Elaine St. Johns, *Prayer Can Change Your Life,* 17th ed. [Engelwood Cliffs, N.J.: Prentice-Hall, 1965], pp. 244-45.)

Jesus never said, "If you try to draw near to me, then I will receive you when you finally get here." He never intended to be only a destination but also to be our companion and guide along the way.

As we slowly learn and grow, he will patiently lead us through all we need to experience as we prepare to return to the Father. As we turn away from the world, as we let go of our substitutes and take those first timid steps toward the Savior, we will always discover him there, with his loving arms stretched toward us, just as a parent reaches toward its child when it is learning to walk.

It seems to me that there is a parallel between Peter's problem and the struggle we have with our Goliaths. Remember the terrible anguish he felt when Christ told him he would deny him that very night? Peter was so sure of himself, so confident in his faithfulness and devotion, that he actually dared to contradict Christ's prophecy, vowing that he would die before he would deny him. And yet he denied him three times. He was heartbroken.

Peter could not become the great and powerful leader that Jesus knew he could be until he learned the bitter lesson we all need to learn — that none of us can ever become good enough for Heavenly Father without the Savior's help in the becoming.

Once Peter discovered his inadequacy, his pride was broken. I doubt if Peter saw it as pride; I'm sure he thought it was devotion. Peter was then able to surrender his desire for self-sufficiency to the humble dependence upon Christ that the Savior taught in the analogy of "the child to the parent" and "the branch to the vine." (See Matt. 18:3 and John 15:1-5.)

Those who make Christ the center and foundation of their lives and then live in obedience to his gospel are guaranteed exaltation. Yes, guaranteed! This is to say that no evil, no sin, no weakness, no Goliath, nothing shall be strong enough to overcome those who truly make Jesus "the way" that they follow. As he said, "I am Messiah, the King of Zion, the Rock of Heaven, which is broad as eternity; *whoso cometh in at the gate and climbeth up by me shall never fall.*" (Moses 7:53; emphasis added.)

As Helaman told his sons, "Remember, remember that it is upon the rock of our Redeemer, who is Christ, the Son of God, that ye must build your foundation; that when the devil shall send forth his mighty winds, yea, his shafts in the whirlwind, yea, when all his hail and his mighty storm shall beat upon you, it shall have no power over you to drag you down to the gulf of misery and endless wo, because of the rock upon which ye are built, which is a sure foundation, *a foundation whereon if men build they cannot fall."* (Hel. 5:12; emphasis added.)

It doesn't matter how we got where we are. The way out remains the same: Jesus Christ—for he is the Way. And we don't have to have *all* the answers when we know the one who is *the* Answer.

THE DIVINE
PARTNERSHIP

Elder Marion D. Hanks once told of a youngster who was assigned by his father to remove a large rock from the yard. The little boy tugged and pushed and lifted and struggled, but all to no avail. Even when he enlisted the help of his neighborhood buddies, the boulder would not budge. Reluctantly he reported to his father that he could not move the rock.

"Have you done all you could?" asked the father.

"Yes," said the boy.

"Are you sure you have tried everything?" the father persisted.

"Yes, I've tried everything."

"No, son, you haven't tried everything. You haven't asked me for help."

Then Elder Hanks observed, "Some of us may be less happy than we could be because of arrogance or pride. We think we are sufficient unto ourselves. We think we do not need God or his Christ. Why do so many of us 'heirs of God, joint-heirs with Christ,' fail to go to him? He is anxious to help. But he wants us to learn our need for him." (*Ensign*, July 1972, p. 105.)

The world has taught us to glorify the achievements of the "self-made" person, but the purpose of the gospel is to lead us into a new birth, by which we become a Christ-made man or woman.

For centuries theologians have debated whether people are saved by grace or by works. The truth is that it is not an either-or choice. Overcoming our spiritual problems is supposed to be a partnership between our best efforts and God's grace and power, which expand and strengthen and even make possible our efforts. Somehow, his grace enables us to do what we righteously choose to do but lack the full ability to accomplish by ourselves. Several verses of scripture describe this divine partnership:

> We labor diligently to write, to persuade our children, and also our brethren, to believe in Christ, and to be reconciled to God; for we know that it is by grace that we are saved, after all we can do. (2 Ne. 25:23.)

> If it so be that the children of men keep the commandments of God [in other words — if we do our part to the best of our ability, then] he doth nourish them, and strengthen them, and *provide means* whereby they can accomplish the thing which he has commanded them. (1 Ne. 17:3; emphasis added.)

What "strength and means" does he provide? Whatever is required. It might be that we need additional patience, compassion, or selflessness. Perhaps we need additional knowledge, courage, or teaching ability. The promise is that whatever we need after doing our best with the ability we do have, his grace is sufficient to take us the rest of the way.

A pioneer related: "I have pulled my handcart when I was so weak and weary from illness and lack of food that I could hardly put one foot ahead of the other. I have looked ahead and seen a patch of sand and I have said, 'I can only go that far and then I must give up, for I cannot pull the load through it.' I have gone on to that sand and when I reached it, the cart began pushing me. I have looked back many times to see who was pushing my cart, but my eyes saw no one, and I knew then that the angels of God were there." ("The Refiner's Fire," *Ensign,* May 1979, p. 53.)

We don't pull handcarts anymore, but we all have Goliaths

to fight, we all have burdens to bear. God has promised that when we do our part, to the best of our ability, be it great or small, he will magnify our effort and make us equal to the task if we will allow it.

No matter what our sins are, no matter how heavy our guilt, no matter how long we have struggled with our bad habits, our problems, or even our addictions, Jesus Christ will meet us there, right at the point of our need. He will help us fight our battles, no matter what they are. With him as our partner, we can all break free and find victory.

When we doubt ourselves, we are really doubting the Savior, who said, "My grace is sufficient." (Ether 12:27.) President Ezra Taft Benson emphasized this when he said of the Savior: "He possesses all the attributes of the divine nature of God. . . . If we are weak or deficient in any of these qualities, he stands willing to strengthen and compensate. Because he descended below all things, he knows how to help us rise above our daily difficulties. Indeed there is no human condition—be it suffering, incapacity, inadequacy, mental deficiency, or sin— which he cannot comprehend or for which his love will not reach out to the individual." ("Jesus Christ: Our Savior and Redeemer," *Ensign,* November 1983, pp. 6-8.)

Just before Jesus left the Church in the hands of the apostles, just prior to his ascension into heaven, almost the last words out of his mouth were: "All power is given unto me in heaven and in earth." (Matt. 28:18.)

Why would he want that to be remembered as his parting words? Perhaps so we would understand that it doesn't matter to him what our Goliath is, or how long it has enslaved us, or how helpless we are, because his power is infinite, both in heaven and on earth, right here where we are fighting the battle. He was telling us that he has all the power required to free us, to perfect us; that we don't need to fail over and over; that he doesn't expect us to do it by ourselves.

The word *power* occurs in scripture over eight hundred times! Indeed, the message that God has the power to help us fight our battles is almost synonymous with the gospel.

In 1 Corinthians 4:20, Paul said, "The kingdom of God is not in word, but in power."

In 1 Corinthians 2:5, he said, "Your faith should not stand in the wisdom of men, but in the power of God."

And in Romans 1:16, he wrote: "I am not ashamed of the gospel of Christ: for it is the power of God unto salvation to everyone that believeth." Believeth in what? In the power of Christ to free us — to lift, expand, and perfect us.

We believe that Jesus changed the water into wine, so why are we hesitant to believe in his power to change us? We believe that he magnified a few loaves of bread and fishes to meet the needs of thousands. Why is it so hard to believe that he can magnify our efforts until we gain the victory over our Goliaths?

"*All power* is given unto me in heaven and in earth."

A woman who was working her way out of difficult circumstances once said to me: "I felt so alone and helpless. I thought that because I had gotten myself into this situation, I did not have the right to ask for help to get out of it."

Haven't we all had that feeling? And that's exactly how Satan wants us to feel so that we won't draw upon the Savior's power. She continued: "The thing that has helped me the most is learning that I can't do it alone. It is such a relief to know that I am not expected to."

An elder I knew in the Air Force told me of an experience he had as a missionary on an Indian reservation. Everywhere the elders went, the Protestant ministers followed, trying to confuse the investigators and counteract their teachings.

One elderly woman was very devout and deeply desired to know the truth. But she was torn between the teachings of the missionaries and the claims of the ministers.

One night she had a dream in which God was waiting for her at the top of a mountain she was trying to climb. However, she was old and weak, and when she had climbed only a short distance, she stopped and wept because she could go no further. Then, in her dream, the two ministers came along and said, "Let us help you." But about halfway up the mountain, the two ministers suddenly let go of her arms and turned to go back down the mountain. Alarmed, she asked why they were leaving her. They told her they had taken her as far as they could go. Greatly disappointed, she turned back and looked up toward the top of the mountain, where she saw the two elders who had been teaching her coming down from the top to take her up the rest of the way.

We all have spiritual mountains to climb, and if we are willing to do all that is within our limited power, we will always find the grace and power to go the rest of the way coming down to us from the Lord above. President Spencer W. Kimball promised: "In abandoning evil, transforming lives, changing personalities, molding characters or remolding them, we need the help of the Lord, and we may be assured of it if we do our part.

"The man who leans heavily upon his Lord becomes the master of self and can accomplish anything he sets out to do, whether it be to secure the brass plates, build a ship, overcome a habit, or conquer a deep-seated transgression." (*The Miracle of Forgiveness* [Salt Lake City: Bookcraft, 1969], p. 176.)

If ever someone might have had a right to take credit for his righteousness, surely it was Enoch, who was translated. And yet he said to the Lord, "Thou hast made me, and given unto me a right to thy throne, *and not of myself, but through thine own grace.*" (Moses 7:59; emphasis added.)

An elder at the Missionary Training Center was failing in his language studies. He complained to his instructor, "I study constantly. I've tried the hardest I know how, but I still can't learn it. It's just too hard for me, so I'm going home."

The wise instructor replied, "Your trouble is that you don't spend enough time on your knees."

The elder repented of trying to accomplish this sacred assignment by himself. Once he allowed the Lord to become his partner in the task, he not only learned the language but left the MTC at the top of his group.

This elder's experience draws us to this important caution: Jesus Christ "is able to do exceeding abundantly above all that

we ask or think, *according to the power that worketh in us.*"
(Eph. 3:20; emphasis added.)

The Lord has things planned for our progress and joy that
we cannot even conceive, but his ability to work these "exceedingly abundant" blessings in our life is dependent upon
or "according to" the power that dominates our life. Let's think
about that for a moment. What power is in us? The power to
perfect ourselves? No, not without divine assistance. The
power to obey without mistakes? No, only Christ has done
that. Is it willpower? No. This is a desirable power. But if it
is all we use to overcome our undesirable behaviors, our otherwise acceptable effort toward self-sufficiency can become a
false God. And it will prevent the divine partnership between
our best efforts and God's grace — the only way we can proceed
to total victory.

Jesus Christ "is able to keep you from falling, and to present you faultless before the presence of his glory with exceeding joy." (Jude 1:24.) But he can do this only if *his* power
is dominant in our lives.

The Lord said that people "should be anxiously engaged
in a good cause, and do many things of their own free will, and
bring to pass much righteousness; *for the power is in them,*
wherein they are agents unto themselves." (D&C 58:27-28;
emphasis added.)

What power is in them? The power to choose! And one of
our most important choices should be to allow Christ's power
to have dominion in our day-to-day battles. Because Jesus
cannot fail, the only reason for us to fail in conquering our
Goliaths is because we are too dependent upon ourselves and
not sufficiently dependent upon him.

The Savior taught that, at the day of judgment, each of our
lives will be reviewed to see what we have done for him, in
response to what he has done for us. (See Matt. 25:31-46 and
Rev. 20:12, for example.) But I think we should also expect to
be judged by what we have allowed Jesus Christ to do for us.
The Savior spoke often of the importance of a broken heart
and contrite spirit, and of the need to rely upon him and his

words. I expect our lives will be examined to see if we were willing to admit our need for him and throw ourselves upon his grace and mercy, or if we allowed our pride to keep us struggling throughout our life with self-sufficiency and will-power alone.

Elder Hugh W. Pinnock has said: "We function best in an environment of freedom. We are free when we are independent, *and we are totally independent only when we are completely dependent upon the Savior.*" (*BYU Devotional Speeches of the Year* [Provo, Utah: Brigham Young University Press, 1979], p. 116; emphasis added.)

As President Benson has noted: "Faith in Him is more than mere acknowledgment that He lives. It is more than professing belief. Faith in Jesus Christ consists of complete reliance on Him." ("Jesus Christ: Our Savior and Redeemer," *Ensign,* November 1983, p. 8.)

GOD IS ALWAYS PREPARED

When David went to challenge Goliath, the Lord influenced him to pause at the brook that ran between the two armies and to select "five smooth stones" for his sling. (1 Sam. 17:40.)

As I have thought about the many years that it takes to smooth a stone so that it is just the right size and shape for a sling, I have come to see those five stones as symbols. I like to think of them as tokens of the planning and foresight God uses to prepare the solutions to our problems and to have the resources in place at the exact time and place we will someday need them.

I'm sure that Satan would challenge the significance of David's stones. He would want to distract us from God's influence by pointing out that there are smooth stones in every stream, which is true, but let us not forget who created them. The point is that God has infinite resources available for our use. Of course he has smooth stones in every stream, just as he has prepared the solutions and answers to every problem. He has placed resources all around us, ready and waiting for our need to arise.

Nothing will ever come into our lives that will catch the Lord off guard. Nothing that can happen to us will ever surprise the Lord or find him unprepared to fill our needs. As Paul wrote: "My God shall supply all your need according to his riches in glory by Christ Jesus." (Philip. 4:19.) And Mormon wrote: "I do not know all things; but the Lord knoweth all things which are to come; wherefore, he worketh in me to do according to his will." (W. of M. 1:7.)

With perfect knowledge and ability to see our future needs, Heavenly Father and Jesus invest much time and effort preparing solutions and resources that will be ready to appear in our lives at the exact time and place we will need them to do battle with our Goliaths. The word *prepare* and its derivatives are used in scripture over four hundred times! For example: "The Lord knoweth all things from the beginning; wherefore, *he prepareth a way* to accomplish his works among the children of men; for behold, he hath all power unto the fulfilling of all his words." (1 Ne. 9:6; emphasis added.)

"If it so be that the children of men keep the commandments of God he doth nourish them, and strengthen them, *and provide means* whereby they can accomplish the thing which he has commanded them." (1 Ne. 17:3; emphasis added.)

President Thomas S. Monson told a story about a stake conference in Grand Junction, Colorado, that illustrates the power of the Lord to prepare resources. In the conference were a grieving mother and father whose son had barely arrived in the mission field. I don't know if he was frightened or what his problem was, but he had quickly announced his intention to return home.

After the conference, Elder Monson met with the parents and knelt in prayer. As he prayed, he could hear the muffled sobs of the heartbroken parents. When they arose, the father asked Elder Monson if he really thought Heavenly Father could somehow alter their son's decision to return home without completing his mission.

"Where is your son serving?" asked Elder Monson.

The father replied, "In Dusseldorf, Germany."

Elder Monson put his arms around the couple and spoke these amazing words: "Your prayers have been heard and are already being answered. With more than twenty-eight stake conferences being held this day, attended by the General Authorities, I was assigned to your stake today. Of all the Brethren, I am the only one who has the assignment to meet with the missionaries in the Dusseldorf Germany Mission this very Thursday." (*Ensign*, May 1978, p. 21.)

I knew a man who joined the Church but continued to have doubts about it. He loved the Church and came to all the meetings, but as problems came into his life, he really struggled to make up his mind whether the Church was true or not.

As my friend was driving his car one day, this burden of doubt pressed forcefully down upon him. He cried out to the Lord to please erase his doubt and reveal the truth to him once and for all. After his prayer, he reached over and turned on the radio just in time to hear the announcer say: "Our next song will be the 'Battle Hymn of the Republic,' sung by the Mormon Tabernacle Choir." As they sang, the Spirit flowed through him, giving the witness that he had asked for.

This raises some interesting questions: When did God prepare the answer to that prayer? Was it just a coincidence that the radio was already tuned to the right station to hear that particular song? Was it a coincidence that the disc jockey chose that song at that precise moment? Did God perhaps have this man's future prayer in mind clear back when He prompted the director of the choir to make that recording? It really doesn't make any difference, once we know that God is always in control; that we will never catch him unprepared; that we will never catch him off guard or surprise him with a need he is not prepared to supply.

"The Lord is my shepherd; I shall not want." (Ps. 23:1.)

THE ATONEMENT

I received a call from a friend one day, asking Sister Cramer and me to come over to her home and talk with a young woman who was in trouble. We learned that this girl was visiting from an out-of-state college. Butterfly is what we call her now. By the end of my story you'll understand why.

When Butterfly left home to start college, she fell in with the wrong crowd and became involved in drugs and alcohol. At first it seemed fun and exciting, but as the chemical dependence became more and more demanding, she realized that she was out of control and that she had better turn things around. She tried to start a program of repentance but discovered that she had indulged too long. Not only was her body addicted to the chemicals but also to the stimulation and emotional escape they afforded as a way to cope with her empty feelings of worthlessness.

School counselors, loving friends, and bishops all worked with this beautiful daughter of God, but she only sank deeper and deeper. To those who were trying to help her, it must have seemed that she was bent upon self-destruction. So, by the time we met Butterfly, she really was in trouble. She said she wanted to change her life, but she had tried and failed so many times that she felt trapped in the depths of despair and hopelessness. When I tried to talk with her about God, she replied angrily that she didn't believe in God anymore, but if she ever found out that there is a God, the only thing she would feel for him would be hatred! I didn't know what to say.

In my heart I cried out, "Heavenly Father, what do you want me to say to this girl? What can I do to reach her? I need to know now!" Immediately an answer came into my mind. "Tell her how you feel about my Son." And so I did.

First, I told her about my own battle with sin, because that is how I came to know the Savior. I described how hopeless I had felt because nothing I tried worked for me. I explained that no matter how hard I fought, things just continued to get worse, and I came to hate myself so much that I could no longer stand to live with what I had become.

I related how the Savior had reached into my life and rescued me through the power of his atonement. He freed me from all the pain and guilt, and as I learned to put him first in my life, he gave me the strength to overcome my evil habits. As he blessed me with an overwhelming love for him and the Heavenly Father, he literally changed my heart and my nature.

Then I talked with Butterfly about the atonement and how it had changed my life. I reminded her that the torture inflicted upon Jesus began late Thursday night after a mob of cutthroats, led by the traitor Judas, bound him and dragged him from the Garden of Gethsemane like a common criminal.

We discussed how he was illegally judged and condemned by false witnesses; how all night long they made sport with him; how he was beaten, taunted, ridiculed. They beat upon him with their fists; they ripped the hair of his beard from his cheeks; they spit in his face.

Early the next morning they took Jesus to Pilate, who had him scourged and condemned him to death. I explained a Roman scourging to her—how they stripped the victim of his clothes and tied him to a post; how they beat him with a *flagra*, a whip with long leather strips. I told her that to make the beating more severe, they tipped each strip with bits of jagged bone or bent nails so the whip would cut and tear into the flesh.

As the bloodthirsty soldiers gathered around to watch Jesus suffer, the soldier with the whip drew back and struck! A deep gash was cut into the Savior's back, and the blood began to flow. Then came another blow, and another and another until his muscles were laid bare and his back, sides, and shoulders were literally shredded raw, and the stripes, foreseen by Isaiah, were placed upon his back. (See Isaiah 53.) Often, a Roman scourging was so brutal that the prisoner died before it was finished.

Meanwhile, as Pilate squirmed under the dilemma of what to do with this innocent man, his soldiers entertained themselves by mocking the "King of the Jews." Upon his raw and bloody flesh they hung the purple robe that Herod had previously draped upon him in ridicule. They made him a crown of thorns and pounded it into his head with a rod, causing the blood to stream down his face. They put the rod in his hand as a scepter. (See Matt. 27:28-30; James E. Talmage, *Jesus The Christ* [Salt Lake City: Deseret Book Company, 1956], p. 639.)

I wonder which hurt Christ the most—the physical pain or the insults of the soldiers, for whom and by whom he was suffering, as they bowed before him, spitting in his face and mocking him as King of the Jews.

Next they took Jesus into the street and forced him to carry his own cross. I asked Butterfly to visualize the effect of the rough beam on his wounded shoulders as he tried to bear its weight. I asked her to consider the effort it must have required to hold the cross away from his head, so as not to drive the thorny crown further into his scalp. Soon he stumbled and collapsed under the weight of his burden. What was it like as that heavy beam crushed his exhausted body into the dusty street?

By the time they reached the top of the hill, the blood from his back and shoulders would probably have dried and glued the robe to his raw flesh. Jews are crucified naked, however, so his clothing was ripped away, reinjuring his bleeding wounds.

Eager to be about their work, the soldiers pushed his bleeding back against the rough cross and drove iron spikes through his hands and feet.

And then something remarkable happened. We read that

he prayed: "Father, forgive them for they know not what they do." And suddenly, instead of being drawn to his mercy, we find barriers erected between us and his forgiveness as our guilty conscience protests, *Yes, he could forgive them, because they didn't know better. But I do know that I'm doing wrong, and yet, because of my weakness, I continue to do it over and over again. So how could I ever expect him to forgive me?*

How many times have we sat in church, in a conference, or in the temple, and felt the Holy Spirit burning in us, filling us with an overwhelming desire to go forth and do mighty things, to draw closer to God, only to face the crushing guilt that comes as we waver before the next temptation that Satan throws in our path? We hate ourselves for our weakness. It makes us feel inadequate, as if the gospel is just too hard for us to live. And we feel so much shame that, for days, we go without praying to that perfect and holy God we were trying to please.

What a strange paradox that our best intentions can become the very things that lead to our defeat. It can really be discouraging, but *that* is why he suffered for us. That is why we all need the grace and atonement of Jesus Christ; to save us from ourselves, and to help us reach beyond the limitations of our own abilities.

Today, all over the world, our embassies are being barricaded to prevent intrusion by terrorists. Even in America, concrete barriers have been placed across the entries to the White House. But the problem Butterfly had is the same that many of us have. Instead of building spiritual barriers to protect us and keep Satan out of our lives, we surround ourselves with emotional barriers to hide behind and keep God from getting too close.

Satan works diligently to magnify these barriers in our minds and hearts because he knows that as we become negative and pessimistic, our mental and emotional energy drains away, leaving us feeling empty and stripped of the will to fight back. We lose confidence that God cares about us. We stop praying. We doubt his power and even his willingness to deliver us.

Some of the people who suffer from such barriers have expressed their feelings to me, feelings such as:

"I sincerely feel that I am not worth salvaging."

"I feel lower than slime. I wonder if I will ever be worthy to rub shoulders with real people again."

"I feel like a failure in all avenues of my life. I feel totally isolated and cut off from all hope for the future."

"I feel like I am dirtying the chapel when I go to church."

"I long for the feeling of nothing. The pain continues to mount with no letup in sight. Daily I pray for death to overtake me."

"After what I have done, I have no right to ask anyone for help, especially God."

I could quote these kinds of statements by the dozen, and so could every bishop and stake president, because, from time to time, almost everyone goes through those kinds of feelings. That is why we must be careful what kinds of barriers we build. Butterfly almost destroyed her eternal destiny by erecting the wrong kind.

Butterfly didn't realize the kind of barriers she was hiding behind, but one thing she made plain! She didn't want anything more to do with religion or empty platitudes. She hurt inside, and she needed answers that worked, answers that could free her. This she began to glimpse in the atonement. She was moved by the things we had discussed. But I wanted her to understand that even though the physical suffering Jesus endured was terrible, even unthinkable, it all pales to insignificance when compared to the suffering he had already endured in the Garden of Gethsemane the night before. "What was it he encountered there that could be worse than this?" Butterfly wanted to know.

I explained that when Jesus entered the garden that night, he came as the perfect lamb, for though he had suffered many temptations, he had never once given in. Until he entered the

garden that night, Jesus did not know what it was like to feel
guilty or ashamed! (Heb. 4:15; Mosiah 15:5; D&C 20:22.)

Robert L. Millet has written: "Jesus, Creator and Jehovah,
surely had known for a long time what He must do. Nevertheless, *He had never known, personally, the exquisite and ex-
acting process of an atonement before.* And it was so much worse
than even He with His unique intellect had ever imagined."
(*Ensign,* December 1986, p. 26; emphasis added.)

The scriptures reveal that as Jesus began to assume the
guilt and punishment for our sins, and as the unfamiliar feelings
of shame and unworthiness suddenly began to crush down
upon him, he was stunned! For example, Mark reports that
he was "sore amazed and . . . very heavy." (Mark 14:33.) The
Greek translation of this phrase is that Jesus was "awestruck
and astonished." Elder Neal A. Maxwell described the Lord's
astonishment in these words: "He had been intellectually and
otherwise prepared from ages past for this task. He is the
Creator of this and other worlds. He knew the plan of salvation.
He knew this is what it would come to. *But when it happened,
it was so much worse than even he had imagined!*" (*Ensign,*
August 1986, p. 14.)

As Jesus left the apostles to go a little deeper into the
garden, he suddenly collapsed under the weight of our sins.
The burden was so heavy that he fell on his face. (Matt. 26:39.)
His agony was so great that huge drops of blood were forced
from his pores. (Luke 22:44.) F. W. Farrar noted: "Then came
the agony in the garden, which filled Him with speechless
amazement and shuddering, until He had to fling Himself with
His face to the earth in the tense absorption of prayer, and
His sweat was like great gouts of blood streaming to the
ground." (Quoted in Bruce R. McConkie, *The Mortal Messiah*
[Salt Lake City: Deseret Book Company, 1981], 4:231.)

Elder Bruce R. McConkie wrote: "The agonies of Gethsemane have seen the blood of a God fall in oozing drops from
every pore to hallow forever that sacred spot, where, among
the olive trees, apart even from his intimate friends, he took
upon himself that weight which none other could bear. His

blood, the choicest blood on earth, the atoning blood of God's Son, is now dried on the rocks and mingled with the soil of the Garden where the greatest miracle of the ages has been wrought." (*The Mortal Messiah,* 4:128-29.)

I suggested to Butterfly that we can better understand why this happened if we think about how it feels to be blamed and punished for something we did not do. Jesus was perfectly innocent of any sin. Yet, in the Garden of Gethsemane that night, as he began the atonement, he suffered the effects of our sins exactly the same as if he had committed them himself. (Alma 7:11-13; Isa. 53:3-5.) Thus, for the first time in his life, as he bore our punishment, he personally felt and experienced what it is like to be unclean and ashamed to pray. He learned what it is like to feel worthless and to despise yourself for your filthiness.

Susan T. Mitchell wrote: "One day as I was pondering the meaning of what occurred in Gethsemane, the thought came to me that the Savior had indeed experienced what I felt. We are told that he suffered for our sins. *Since one of the sufferings caused by sin is a loss of self-esteem, it is likely that he felt, among other things, the full weight of our own self-condemnation.*" ("And I Should Heal Them," *Ensign,* April 1981, p. 14; emphasis added.)

Elder James E. Talmage felt that this exposure to the painful barriers that separate us from Heavenly Father literally broke his heart. (*Jesus the Christ,* p. 669; also Ps. 69:20.) Paul said that it caused Christ to weep for us "with strong crying and tears." (Heb. 5:7.)

The price that Christ paid there in the garden and again on the cross was infinite, because it paid the penalty demanded by justice for every sin that ever had been or would yet be committed. Knowing that Butterfly was nearly destroyed by the pain of her failure and self-loathing, I wanted her to realize that if she could somehow add up the total amount of guilt and pain and sorrow and fear and suffering that she had felt in her entire life, and then feel that all at one time, that is what Jesus endured there in the garden—for her, for me, for you—for every person in the world combined! We know this is so because Jacob said: "He cometh into the world that he may save all men if they will hearken unto his voice; for behold, *he suffereth the pains of all men, yea, the pains of every living creature, both men, women, and children, who belong to the family of Adam.*" (2 Ne. 9:21; emphasis added.)

President Marion G. Romney interpreted that scripture to mean that the suffering he endured "equalled the combined suffering of all men," and that "no man nor set of men nor all men put together ever suffered what the Redeemer suffered in the Garden." (*When Thou Art Converted, Strengthen Thy Brethren*, 1974-75 Melchizedek Priesthood Manual [Salt Lake City: The Church of Jesus Christ of Latter-day Saints, 1974], p. 47.)

President John Taylor wrote: "The suffering of the Son of God was not simply the suffering of personal death; for in assuming the position that He did in making an atonement for the sins of the world *He bore the weight, the responsibility, and the burden of the sins of all men, which, to us, is incomprehensible.*" (*The Mediation and Atonement* [Salt Lake City: Deseret News Company, 1882], p. 150; emphasis added.)

I wasn't sure Butterfly understood the significance of what I had described, so I tried to explain it this way. The pain and punishment Jesus endured was not only *infinite*, it was also *finite* and specific and detailed, focused on each person's individual pain. For example, right there in the garden, Jesus was bearing Butterfly's burden, exactly the same burden she was experiencing almost two thousand years later. As Elder A. Theodore Tuttle said, "There is no pain He did not experience, nor any anguish through which we may pass that he did not know." (*Devotional Speeches of the Year* [Provo, Utah: Brigham Young University Press, 1983-84], p. 41.) Elder Neal A. Maxwell stated: "In ways we cannot comprehend, our sicknesses and infirmities were borne by Him even before these were borne by us." (*Ensign*, November 1981, p. 8.)

Somehow, there in the garden and again on the cross, the Savior looked forward and backward through the corridors of time and viewed the life and sins of every person to live upon this planet. And then, person by person, sin by sin, he paid a price that was infinite in its totality but finite and specific in its detailed pain. (See Bruce R. McConkie, *The Mortal Messiah,* 4:232.)

Robert L. Millet wrote: "The cumulative weight of all mortal sins, somehow, past, present, and future, pressed upon that perfect, sinless, and sensitive soul! All infirmities and sicknesses were part, too, of the awful arithmetic of the Atonement." (*Ensign,* December 1986, p. 26; see also Alma 7:11-13; Isa. 53:3-5; Matt. 8:17.)

I emphasized to Butterfly that if we could understand nothing else about the atonement, we must at least remember that it was not for *"the sins of the world"* that Jesus suffered and died, it was not for "us," nor even for *"all of mankind."* Rather, it was for *her,* for *me,* for *each* person, and what a difference it makes in our lives when we view it that way. It is equally important to know that Jesus Christ not only suffered and died *for* each person, but also *because of* each person. What he suffered in the garden and again on the cross was measurably harder because Butterfly was included, because you and I were included. President Joseph Fielding Smith summarized it this way: "There isn't one of us ... that hasn't done something wrong and then been sorry and wished we hadn't. Then our consciences strike us and we have been very, very, miserable. Have you gone through that experience? I have. . . . But here we have the Son of God carrying the burden of *my* transgressions and *your* transgressions and the transgressions of every soul that receives the gospel of Jesus Christ. *I added something to it; so did you.* So did everybody else." (*The Life and Teachings of Jesus and His Apostles,* 1978 Church Educational System Course Manual, Rel. 211-212 [Salt Lake City: The Church of Jesus Christ of Latter-day Saints, 1978], pp. 175-76; emphasis added.)

Through the shedding of Christ's blood, we were each "bought with a price" (1 Cor. 6:20), and when we come to him in repentance, he knows exactly what our sins cost him in suffering. Because he knows the weight of our burdens, the enormity of our debt, and because of his infinite love for each person, he wants to spare us from having to pay that price, which he already paid, by offering us the forgiveness that justice now allows, contingent upon our repentance and obedience. (D&C 19:16-17; for further detail on the resolution of our guilt, see chapter 12 of this book.)

President Spencer W. Kimball said: "When we think of the great sacrifice of our Lord Jesus Christ and the sufferings he endured for us, we would be ingrates if we did not appreciate it so far as our power made it possible. He suffered and died for us, and yet if we do not repent, *all his anguish and pain on our account are futile.*" (*The Miracle of Forgiveness* [Salt Lake City: Bookcraft, 1969], p. 145; emphasis added.)

Ultimately, then, it is not how much we *understand* of the atonement that brings us to Christ, but how we *feel* and how we respond. The gratitude, the reverence and awe for the Savior's sacrifice that I want to feel is portrayed in an experience of Enoch Waring, while supervising the construction of a chapel on the Tongan Islands. He said that everyone was eager to help, including a little woman over one hundred years old:

> She was on the job the next morning helping to fill the water barrels and carry the brick, which were made out of coral.
>
> I told the little old lady not to carry the water, that the men would do that, so she started to carry the brick. I asked her only to carry one at a time, as they were about the size of our cinder block; but I noticed as soon as I would get out of sight she would be carrying two bricks again.
>
> One of the Tongan men came to me and asked if I had some gloves that the little old lady could wear, as her hands were bleeding. I got down from the building, took my interpreter, and told her again only carry one brick at a time, and then I took off my gloves and gave them to her to wear. The tears started down her cheeks, and I thought that I had wounded her feelings again, and then tears started down my

interpreter's face. He told me that the little old lady was
telling us that the Savior's hands had bled for her, and she
was not ashamed to have her hands bleed for the Savior's
work. (Margie Calhoun Jensen, *When Faith Writes the Story*
[Salt Lake City: Bookcraft, 1973], p. 25.)

When we arrived at my friend's house, we had found Butterfly so wound up with tension and anxiety that she was
wringing her hands and wiggling all over the couch. However,
as we talked, she grew calm. Hearing about the atonement
had cracked those barriers just enough for her to consider the
possibility that someday, somehow, she too might be able to
find what I had found in Jesus Christ.

In the next few months, as Butterfly came to understand
more of Christ's atonement and love, she regained her faith
and testimony, she gave up her bad associations and conquered
her addiction to drugs and alcohol. But most important of all,
she discovered and accepted the love of her Savior and Heavenly Father, who had been right there with her through all
those dark years, waiting for the day when she would finally
open her heart to their healing influence. She sent us a beautiful testimony: "For a long time I had abandoned hope of ever
really changing . . . but then I realized I needed to trust my life
into the hands of a much greater power than that of man on
earth, so I turned to the Lord.

"The past few years have been those of confinement, like
being in a tight cocoon.

"The dark surrounds you, and you wonder if you will ever
see the light again and then when you do, it is so bright that
you almost have to shade your eyes, yet you don't want to
because it is so warm and inviting after such a long time in
the cold darkness."

Now you know why we call this sweet girl Butterfly.

SPARROWS AND PINPRICKS

The size of the universe that God has created is beyond our comprehension. It contains "worlds without number." (Moses 1:33.) Even the galaxy we live in is so large that it cannot be measured in miles. It is measured in light years. Light travels approximately 186,000 miles per second. Thus, a light year is the distance that light travels in one year, going eleven million miles per minute! Our galaxy is shaped something like two plates or pie tins placed face to face. The size of our galaxy is about 10,000 light years deep and 100,000 light years across.

With the giant telescopes now at our command, astronomers have probed over a billion light years in all directions, and everywhere they look are more galaxies. They now estimate that the space they have probed could contain over one hundred million galaxies like ours, with at least a million inhabitable worlds in each one. Moses wrote: "Were it possible that man could number the particles of the earth, yea, millions of earths like this, *it would not be a beginning to the number of thy creations.*" (Moses 7:30; emphasis added.)

Here we learn that if it were possible that we mortals could somehow number every grain of sand and every individual particle of dust, if we could somehow add up that staggering, incomprehensible number, *it would not even be a beginning* to the number of worlds God has created. And yet, whenever the

Lord reveals himself to us, it is not to impress us with the importance of *his* status, but to teach us the importance of *our* status, the importance of *our* potential and destiny.

But even more incredible than these truths about the majesty and glory of our Heavenly Father is the realization that with all the affairs of those countless billions of worlds to monitor and control, he is so concerned about the details of each person's life as to know even trivial things, such as the exact number of hairs on our head. We cannot change by a single hair without the notice of Heavenly Father and his Son! (Matt. 10:30; D&C 84:80.)

The scriptures also reveal our importance to God when they teach that he actually monitors the thoughts and intents of our hearts daily. He knows what we are thinking and feeling, what our needs are and how he can best help us. (See Matt. 12:36; D&C 33:1; 88:109.)

God's perfect love is infinite and unconditional—the more we learn about it, the harder it is to comprehend. And so Jesus gave a simple statement that would leave no room for misunderstanding, an unmistakable example that should prove their love and concern to even the most skeptical among us.

His statement is recorded in Matthew 10:29: "Are not two sparrows sold for a farthing?" And then, to provide further assurance, he said that not one of them could fall to the ground without the notice of our Heavenly Father.

It seems to me that when Jesus talked about sparrows, he was providing divine assurance that God knows who we are; he knows where we are; he knows what we need; and he cares about us more than we can conceive.

As Ammon said: "Now my brethren, we see that *God is mindful of every people*, whatsoever land they may be in; yea, he numbereth his people, and his bowels of mercy are over all the earth." (Alma 26:37.)

The testimony of Julie Allen also illustrates God's intimate attention. One day, as she was having her morning prayer, she heard her little child call out from its crib, "Momma, Momma." She said that she felt so full of joy and appreciation for her child at that moment that she asked, in her prayer: "Heavenly Father, can you hear her? Isn't she precious? Do you know how I feel when she calls, 'Momma'?"

Immediately the answer came into her mind: *"Yes! That is how I feel when you call 'Father.' "* (*Ensign*, January 1985, p. 67; emphasis added.)

Speaking on the subject of God's love and concern for the individual, Elder Paul H. Dunn said: "We must remember that our struggles here are not too trivial to interest the Lord." And then, after referring to some of the immensities of space that we have just considered, he continued: "When we think that our Lord created all that . . . and understands the immensities of space that only boggle our minds, *we have difficulty believing that his interest could ever devolve on something as minute as our little pain or concerns.*

"Well, our frustrations and disappointments may be just pinpricks in the eternal scheme of things, but *since they do not seem that way to us, they do not seem that way to the Lord.* The Lord is waiting to help you cope if you will lay your human-sized needs at his divine feet." (*Ensign*, May 1979, pp. 7-9; emphasis added.)

How wonderful this doctrine is! *Since our problems and desires do not seem like insignificant pinpricks to us, they do not seem that way to the Lord!*

Back in pioneer days, when Hedwig Stapperfend, from Bountiful, Utah, celebrated her tenth birthday, she was given a beautiful eight-inch hand-painted ball. After the party, she was playing catch when the ball suddenly disappeared from sight. Everyone tried to find the ball, but not even the adults could figure out where it had gone.

When everyone else had given up searching, Hedwig presented the problem to her Heavenly Father, who then revealed to her that the ball was hidden under a large cabbage leaf in the garden. (Norma Clark Larsen, *His Everlasting Love* [Salt Lake City: Horizon Publishers, 1982], vol. 2, p. 76.)

As Elder Dunn said, our frustrations and disappointments may be just pinpricks in the eternal scheme of things, *but since a lost ball did not seem that way to this little girl, it did not seem that way to the Lord.*

What heartaches have we been carrying because we didn't think God would want to be bothered by such trivial matters? We are of much greater value than a lowly sparrow or a lost ball.

Linda Alderman, from Kanab, Utah, found out about the Lord's interest in her problems. Because her husband was not a member of the Church, she attended her meetings without him. Every Sunday her two rowdy children would force her to leave the chapel in order to keep them quiet. She said that each time she maneuvered down the aisle with a loud, wiggling bundle in each arm, she always had the same heartache. She could not hear in the foyer. She wanted so much to stay in the meeting and learn, and each week she worried about how much she was missing.

One Sunday the problem came to a head. Only five minutes into the meeting, the two-year-old began whining. Soon the other child joined in. People began turning to look at her. She felt humiliated, and as she made that trek to the foyer once again, she cried out in her heart: "What's the use?" But as she sat on the sofa caring for her children, the Spirit whispered a message to her that she would never have heard in the chapel: *"Your efforts are not going unnoticed;* they are appreciated. Because you must give up some of the learning you might have received in the meetings — in order to teach your children the proper attitudes and actions — you are given far greater learning capacity in the few quiet moments you have to yourself. Through pondering, you are given the knowledge you may miss, and more." (*Ensign,* March 1982, pp. 46-47; emphasis added.)

Linda's burden was lifted and her heart rejoiced. God knew her! He noticed her frustration! And his grace was flowing into her life in compensation for her worthy sacrifices. Yes, our frustrations and disappointments may be just pinpricks in the eternal scheme of things, *but since Linda's frustrations did not seem that way to her, they did not seem that way to the Lord.*

A visiting teacher in Aurora, Colorado, tells a wonderful story about God revealing to her how to make a dress. In her ward was an elderly woman who had some favorite fabric that she wanted made into a dress, but she could no longer see well enough to sew it herself. Her visiting teacher volunteered to make the dress but found, to her dismay, that there was not quite enough material. Then she found that if she made the cuffs and collar from a contrasting material, there would be just enough—if she made no mistakes.

This sister said that she was very frustrated because she could not get the contrast strip and facing to attach properly to the neck line. After several attempts she knelt by the sewing machine and told the Lord how important it was to her to give this dress to the dear old woman, and how it was being ruined as she picked out the stitches over and over, trying to get the neckline correct. As she resumed her work, the way to attach the cloth was revealed to her, and she was filled with the sweet spirit of God's love as she completed the dress.

This visiting teacher reported that when she presented the dress, the elderly woman cried for joy. It was perfect. It was just what she wanted. And the visiting teacher cried also to learn that with all the vast domains and responsibilities throughout the universe to occupy his attention, Heavenly Father wanted this woman to have her dress and went to the trouble to reveal how it could be made. (*Ensign,* February 1980, p. 57.)

Again, our frustrations and disappointments may be just pinpricks in the eternal scheme of things, *but since a simple dress did not seem that way to this elderly sister, it did not seem that way to the Lord.*

In the same way, the Lord will help you with your needs, for, as Alma told his son Helaman, "by small and simple things are great things brought to pass, . . . and by very small means the Lord doth confound the wise and bringeth about the salvation of many souls." (Alma 37:6-7.)

THE GOLIATH OF A POOR SELF-IMAGE

A battered five-year-old girl was brought to a hospital bruised, bleeding, and with broken bones. The mother was crying, repeating over and over, "I'm sorry, I'm sorry, I didn't mean to hit her so hard." As the nurse held the poor child in her arms, the little girl stopped crying and opened her eyes long enough to say, "My mommy says I'm a bad girl." Then she closed her eyes and died.

Satan intends for us to believe that we are bad; that we are worthless and hopeless; that God couldn't possibly love us the way we are. He will beat us with every temptation and discouragement possible to distort our self-image and limit our relationship to God. This is illustrated by the words of a man who compared his excommunication to mine. He said, "As I heard about your court, and the great love shown by your wife in those dark days, the tears started flowing. Then, as I thought about your conversion, your rebaptism, the restoring of your blessings, and finally, your re-entrance into the temple, I had no control over my emotions. For that to happen to me with my wife seems like a dream too far away to grasp."

And then he said, "With my track record, I'm very afraid the First Presidency is going to be very skeptical about my re-entrance into the church."

Satan has people so confused that almost every person thinks his or her "track record" is the worst. I understand this

48

man's doubt about ever belonging among the Saints again, about ever feeling worthy of the gospel and the temple blessings. I felt that way when I was excommunicated. But it angers me how skillfully Satan detracts us from the infinite power of the Savior's love and atonement, which will cleanse the repentant sinner from even the filthiest of sins, and then bring us back to the Father in spotless beauty and purity.

The danger in this man's attitude is that when we *feel* like an unimportant nobody, we *act* like a nobody. Oh, what a price Jesus paid so that we could all overcome our "track records." He believed in us enough to leave his throne of glory to suffer and die for us, so what right do we have to think we are worthless and unimportant? It is not difficult to believe in ourselves once we discover how much God believes in us.

This man had a poor self-image because he did not understand the Lord's perfect, unconditional, and unwavering love. And, therefore, he had low self-worth. He looked at his past mistakes and reached a wrong conclusion. Satan loves to catch us in that trap, but it is *never* too late to change. No matter how many mistakes lie in our past, God is anxious to help us let go of them and leave the past in the past.

Another clever way that Satan attacks our self-image is through the fanaticism of perfectionism. Sometimes we get so hung up on the eternal goal of attaining perfection that we lose our perspective and create barriers by demanding more of ourselves than God expects. It may be centuries, or even millennia, before we have enough experience and maturity to achieve perfection.

I've never been able to find a timetable attached to the commandment to seek perfection. But there are many encouragers like these: "Ye must *practice* virtue and holiness before me." (D&C 46:33; emphasis added.) The word *practice* shows that God is allowing time to learn, time to grow. "Do not run faster or labor more than you have strength and means." (D&C 10:4.) This means we take things in order, one day at a time, not all at once. "Let us run with patience the race that is set before us." (Heb. 12:1.) And, "Continue in patience until ye are perfected." (D&C 67:13.)

President Barbara Smith said: "Goals are stars to steer by, not sticks to beat yourself with." (*Sunstone,* May 1985, p. 21.)

Since God does not reject or condemn us for having unconquered weaknesses, what right do we have to condemn ourselves? Of course we are eager to improve, but inasmuch as God is allowing us time to grow, we must be humble enough to stop condemning ourselves and not allow our imperfections to distort our self-image and form barriers between us and the Lord.

THE GOLIATH OF THOUGHT CONTROL

All sins start in our thoughts. Therefore, one of Satan's foremost objectives is to draw our thoughts away from God. If we are to conquer our Goliaths, the victory must first be gained in our thoughts, because "as [a person] thinketh in his heart, so is he." (Prov. 23:7.) Another way to express this is simply that *what gets our attention gets us.* How could we possibly do or become what we haven't first chosen in our thoughts? When we control the thought, we control the deed.

No thought is too small to have an effect. If we think about it long enough, we are probably going to do it or become it, because the thoughts upon which we focus our attention are the blueprints of our future reality. We always reap in our physical life what we have been sowing in our mental life. If we have been reaping failure, if our Goliaths are presently victorious, it is because we have been sowing thoughts of failure. *Sowing seeds of doubt and worry in our thoughts is like prayer in reverse.*

David conquered his Goliath because, unlike the fearful soldiers, David's thoughts were not focused on his personal limitations or on the power of Goliath. His attention was focused upon God's power and His promise to fight our battles with us. As long as our personal limitations are the focus of our attention, we will continue to fail.

A story in the fourteenth chapter of Matthew demonstrates

51

both the positive and negative effects of this important principle of thought control. The Savior sent the apostles away in Peter's boat so that He could be alone to pray. They got caught in a storm, and the ship was tossed about by the wind and waves.

When the apostles saw the Savior coming toward them, walking on the water, they were afraid and cried out in fear. But Jesus called to them, "Be of good cheer; it is I; be not afraid." (Matt. 14:27.) Peter, fearful but wanting to go to the Lord, said: "Lord, if it be thou, bid me come unto thee on the water." (Matt. 14:28.) I wonder if he realized what he was asking.

The Lord said simply, "Come," just as he says to everyone, "Come." "And when Peter was come down out of the ship, he walked on the water, to go to Jesus." (Matt. 14:29.)

Peter trusted the Lord. If Jesus said that Peter could come, then Peter believed he could do it. It didn't make any difference that it defied the laws of nature. *As long as Peter's attention was focused on the Savior, he did what no other person had ever done!*

But think about what happened to Peter when he took his attention off the Lord and looked at the opposition. When he saw the boisterous wind, he was afraid and began to sink. Oh, Peter, "what gets your attention gets you."

Peter looked at the waves and perhaps even turned around to look at the boat and his dumbfounded companions. If I can put words in his mouth, Peter probably said something like: "Good grief, what am I doing out here? Who do I think I am? This is impossible. I can't do this!" And down he went.

Don't we do the same thing? We resolve to change a habit or overcome a weakness, to go on a diet — or whatever. And after a few days or weeks or months of success, we say "Hold it. I've never done this well before. I've never gone this long before. I've never kept the pounds off this long before. I'm not this good." And immediately we sink back into our old habits, because "what gets your attention gets you."

We need to do what Peter did: repent real fast. "And beginning to sink, he cried, saying, Lord save me. And immediately Jesus stretched forth his hand, and caught him." (Matt. 14:30-31.) The Lord never plays favorites. Whatever he does for one, he is willing to do for all. When we are ready for him, we will always find him there, reaching down and ready to lift us up, just as he was for Peter.

But most likely, the moment we reach out for the Lord, Satan will also be at our side, whispering that we are not worthy, whispering that we have no right to God's help, trying to take our attention off the Savior. But the Lord is anxious to bring us back to the Father and is perfectly willing to take our unworthy hand, as long as it is offered to him in sincere submission and repentance.

As the "natural man" strives for survival and success, it is normal for him to center his thought and emotion, his confidence and his reliance upon himself. We need to realize, however, that this self-centered philosophy was one of the main points of the anti-Christ doctrine preached by Korihor and others like him.

Korihor taught that reliance upon Jesus Christ "is the effect of a frenzied mind; and this derangement of your minds," he said, "comes because of the traditions of your fathers, which lead you away into a belief of things which are not so." (Alma 30:16.)

As Korihor went about teaching people to rely solely upon themselves rather than upon Christ, he taught the popular and appealing humanistic doctrine that "every man fared in this life according to the management of the creature; therefore every man prospered according to his genius, and that every man conquered according to his [own] strength." (Alma 30:17.) It is this kind of thinking that gives the victory to Goliath.

On the other hand, when we focus our thoughts, faith, and attention upon the fact that Jesus Christ has already overcome every problem that we can possibly face, then we can, through the miracle of his grace, be endowed with the knowledge, the confidence, the hope, and the power to overcome every limitation, every Goliath. As Paul wrote: "For though we walk in the flesh, we do not war after the flesh: (for the weapons of our warfare are not carnal [meaning mortal], but mighty through God to the pulling down of strong holds;) casting down imaginations, and every high thing that exalteth itself against the knowledge of God [such as habits], *and bringing into captivity every thought to the obedience of Christ."* (2 Cor. 10:3-5; emphasis added.)

Here Paul reaffirms that when we put Christ and his promises at the center of our attention, allowing him to become our partner in the battle, we can actually destroy the "strong holds" of habits and even compulsive addictions. Even more exciting is his promise that we can "cast down [evil] imaginations" and bring *every thought* into harmony with Christ. What a promise! When we control the Goliath of thought, we have won the battle.

A common problem of thought that we ourselves create is our mistaken focus on the past. Looking at our past failures, we conclude that we *are* failures. My, how Satan loves that conclusion. It places us in his power instead of Christ's.

The mind is like a magnet. It is polarized by the frequency and the intensity of emotion invested in the thoughts we hold in our attention. So if we are constantly looking backward and condemning ourselves, by that negative focus we unwittingly perpetuate the very thing we were trying to overcome. Thus, in a sense, we become our own worst enemies. The very act of dwelling upon, analyzing, regretting, pondering, and forcing our whole life to revolve around the problem increases its strength and gives it power to dominate us. It could not have that power if we focused our thoughts on Christ and his promises.

Every time we drive a car, we look in the rear-view mirror to see where we have been. No one experiences more misery and unnecessary suffering than those who won't take their attention off the past, insisting on going through life with a rear-view mirror stuck in front of their eyes, always looking back, always digging up the mistakes of the past, dragging them around like a prisoner's ball and chain. Over and over, like a broken record, they relive the past, continually criticizing and condemning themselves for their failures. Surely this does not please the Lord. Elder Marvin J. Ashton said: "Where you've been is not nearly as important as where you are and where you're going." (*This People,* March 1984, p. 27.)

Perhaps we have tried and failed a thousand times. So welcome to the human race. But as long as our past failures remain the focus of our attention, we will continue to fail. As long as we continue to sow thoughts of fear, doubt, and lack of confidence, those are precisely the results we will reap. We can't fix today as long as yesterday is the focus of our attention. Let's get rid of our mental rear-view mirrors. —

Of course, a necessary part of repentance is to look back and acknowledge our mistakes. But what holds our attention holds us, so let's not confuse self-deprecation with repentance. Understand that there comes a time when we must take our eyes off the past and look forward to the redemption of Christ, which erases the past. As Elder Ashton said, "It is a fact of life that *the direction in which we are moving* is more important than where we are." (*Ensign,* May 1987, p. 67; emphasis added.)

Some may ask, "How could I not think about my problem and dwell upon my failure when it blocks my eternal salvation and will destroy me if I don't find a way around it?" I know that question well, for it dominated my life for thirty-two years of defeat. And those thirty-two years would have stretched on and on if I had not learned to take my attention off the problem and center it on the solution — accepting Jesus Christ as my personal Savior.

We place Christ at the center and foundation of our thoughts by learning who he is, what he is, how he feels about our situations and challenges, and how he wants us to respond to them. The will of the Lord and the word of the Lord are one and the same. How can we know the will of God unless we know the word of God? How can we place Christ at the center of our lives if we are ignorant of his word? How can we rely upon the Lord for strength and guidance in time of need if we do not know what he has promised in his scriptures to do for us? Neither the Father nor the Son will ever become familiar to us until we are familiar with their recorded words. As the Lord said: "Whoso receiveth not my voice is not acquainted with my voice, and is not of me. And by this you may know the righteous from the wicked." (D&C 84:52-53.) And king Benjamin noted: "How knoweth a man the master whom he has not served, and who is a stranger unto him, and who is far from the thoughts and intents of his heart?" (Mosiah 5:13.)

Perhaps the most direct path to improving our relationship with God lies in the prayerful study of his revealed word. Jesus indicated that he actually equates our feelings toward his scriptures with our feelings toward him, when he said, "If a man love me, he will keep my words." (John 14:23.) "Keeping his words" means more than obedience. It also means keeping them focused in our thoughts. I am inspired by the words of Job, who said, "I have esteemed the words of his mouth more than my necessary food." (Job 23:12.)

As we learn and then believe the Lord's promises to help us change our hearts and our natures, we will gain new hope and confidence. Surely that is why the Lord said, "You must rely upon my word." (D&C 17:1.)

The Lord expressed a mathematical formula concerning this principle in the sacrament prayers, where we witness to the Father that we are not only "willing to take upon [us] the name" of Christ, but also that we will "*always remember him* and keep his commandments." (D&C 20:77; emphasis added.) The scriptures emphasize that we always reap what we sow. Therefore, the logical reward for holding Christ in our thoughts is "that [we] may always have his Spirit to be with [us]." (D&C 20:77; see also Gal. 6:7.) It is a mathematical ratio: the more we hold him in our thoughts, the more we will have his Spirit to be with us. The less we focus upon him and his scriptural promises, the more room there will be for the problems and temptations of the world to crowd into our mind and pollute our harvest.

In D&C 93:52 the Lord promised: "*Inasmuch as ye keep*

my sayings you shall not be confounded in this world, nor in the world to come." (Emphasis added.) Again it is a ratio: the more we "keep the sayings" focused in our thoughts, the less we will be overcome by the Goliaths of this wicked world. The less attention we pay to the principles and promises, the more easily we are overcome. It is proportionate.

President David O. McKay once said: "What you sincerely in your heart think of Christ will determine what you are, will largely determine what your acts will be." (*Gospel Ideals,* 7th abridged edition [Salt Lake City: Improvement Era Publication, 1953], p. 34.) And the Lord himself commanded: "Look unto me in every thought; doubt not, fear not." (D&C 6:36.)

THE GOLIATH
OF TEMPTATION

An elder in Navy security had the duty of keeping watch over prisoners who were hospitalized. As he made his rounds a couple of days before Christmas, a heavily intoxicated guard invited him to stop and have a drink with him.

The elder said no and was about to continue his rounds when the guard said angrily, "Oh, so you're too good for me!" Suddenly he shoved his pistol in the elder's stomach and said, "You take a drink with me or I'll shoot."

As the elder silently prayed for protection, he again refused.

The guard shoved him into a closet and repeated his threat, to which the elder replied, "I won't drink. You'll have to shoot." The drunken guard couldn't believe it. In disgust he put his gun away and said, "I'm through with you. You're chicken."

Chicken? That's not chicken! That's courage.

Not many of us will be tempted at gunpoint, but nothing will challenge us to battle more often than the Goliath of temptation. As Heber J. Grant said: "There are two spirits striving with us always, one telling us to continue our labor for good, and one telling us that with the faults and failing of our nature we are unworthy. I can truthfully say that from October, 1882, until February, 1883, *that spirit followed me day and night* telling me that I was unworthy to be an Apostle of the Church and I ought to resign." (*Conference Report,* April 1941, pp. 4-6; emphasis added.)

Mormon wrote: "The devil is an enemy unto God, and fighteth against him continually, and inviteth and enticeth to sin, and to do that which is evil continually." (Moro. 7:12.) This means that Satan's forces are working against us twenty-four hours a day, around the clock, around the calendar, around the centuries, until the Lord decrees that the battle is over. In Helaman 13:37 we are told that we are constantly "surrounded by demons, yea, we are encircled about by the angels of him who hath sought to destroy our souls." (See also D&C 76:29.)

Jesus said, "Let the church take heed and *pray always,* lest they fall into temptation." (D&C 20:33; emphasis added.) The Savior would not command us to "pray always" for protection from temptation if he did not expect us to encounter continual temptation throughout mortality. Satan does not tempt us because we are evil. He tempts us because he knows who we are and how good we can become.

We know that Jesus was perfect, but even he "was in *all points* tempted like as we are, yet without sin." (Heb. 4:15; emphasis added.) Was Jesus so holy that it was easy for him to resist these temptations? Was his exposure to temptations "in all points" merely an academic overview, or were they real encounters like ours? The answer from the scriptures is that his resistance to the constant temptation was a major part of his "sufferings."

"He shall go forth, suffering pains and afflictions and temptations of every kind." (Alma 7:11.)

"[He] suffereth temptation, and yieldeth not to the temptation." (Mosiah 15:5.)

Jesus would not have "suffered" in his resistance to temptations unless they were real. Since Jesus was truly tempted, and yet remained sinless, we know that *it is not a sin to feel tempted.*

James said, "Blessed is the man that endureth temptation" (James 1:12), but nowhere do the scriptures say, or even hint, "Blessed is the person who never feels temptation." There is no such person. When we face Christ at the day of judgment, it will not be our temptations that will concern him but the choices we made in response to them.

Temptations are much easier to resist when we regard them as part of "the carnal nature" instead of part of ourselves. Then it becomes "I" resisting "it" instead of "I" resisting "me." When temptations arouse our desires, it is helpful to think of them as winds from Satan, merely blowing past us. We feel them, but they cannot affect us unless we decide to reach out and make them part of our lives. This concept of separation of ourselves from the temptation adds so much power to our ability to resist that we can actually say to ourselves, and mean it: "Yes, that might be fun (or feel good) *but it is not worth it to me!*"

There is a second, more subtle kind of Goliath that can attack us even when we refuse to indulge our temptations. It is the false guilt and derogatory self-image we feel because we waver before we say a final no to the temptation. However, it is not the wavering that is important, but the choice we make and the action we take. We see this in the Savior's life.

During his mortal ministry, the Savior set the perfect example of unwavering obedience. Never once did he falter in submitting his will to the Father — until he reached the Garden of Gethsemane. And there, even he wavered under the crushing weight of our sins. No mortal words can convey the pain that he suffered there, but the agony that caused him to waver was so great that instead of kneeling, he "fell on his face, and prayed, saying, O my Father, if it be possible, let this cup pass from me: nevertheless not as I will, but as thou wilt." (Matt. 26:39.)

Our perfect, flawless Savior felt such pain and desire to escape that he actually repeated that urgent prayer three times! And he wanted this wavering recorded in the description of his life. It is so important for us to know that *he also wavered* that he repeated the account once again in our own time: "Which suffering caused myself, even God, the greatest of all, to tremble because of pain, and to bleed at every pore . . . and would that I might not drink the bitter cup, and shrink — nevertheless, glory be to the Father, and I partook and finished my preparations unto the children of men." (D&C 19:18-19.)

Three reasons come to mind why the Savior might want us to know that he wavered and shrank from his duty.

First, when our mortal weaknesses cause us to waver and shrink from our responsibilities, we can remember that he also had those same feelings. Jesus would have us understand that there is neither shame nor disgrace in having the mortal desire to quit, or to escape the challenges we encounter — not as long, that is, as we endure to the end and continue to pray, in spite of our feelings, "nevertheless not my will, but thine be done." Since the Lord himself had to cry for help, why should we be ashamed when we feel a similar need?

Secondly, we need to remember that when Jesus prayed for strength to resist his wavering commitment, he was not denied the help he needed. Because he *wanted* to resist, because he prayed, "Nevertheless not my will, but thine, be done . . . there appeared an angel unto him from heaven, *strengthening him.*" (Luke 22:42-43; emphasis added.) When our feelings are pulling us from our duty, we too will be given strength to endure if we will only follow his example and ask for help instead of condemning ourselves.

The third message of this sacred account is that we should be totally honest with God about our feelings. The Savior did not try to fake the garden experience. He was in agony, and he found himself shrinking from his duty. He certainly did not want to feel that way, but he was honest enough and humble enough to tell his Father how he really felt and to ask for help not to feel that way.

When we are hurting, when we find our commitment weakening, we should say so in prayer. Why should we allow our foolish pride to cause us to try to hide our feelings from God? He already knows how we feel, and he understands. Heavenly Father did not condemn Jesus or count his wavering as sin. Rather, he sent help to strengthen his resolve and to keep him in the line of his duty, and that is exactly what he will do for us when our hearts are honest and submissive before him.

Alma told us to rely on the Lord: "I would that ye should remember, that as much as ye shall put your trust in God even so much ye shall be delivered out of your trials, and your troubles, and your afflictions, and ye shall be lifted up at the last day." (Alma 38:5.)

It was not by avoiding the realities of life's temptations that the Savior's holiness was perfected. No one ever walked the earth more conscious of sin than Jesus Christ. His holiness and purity came, as should ours, by the resistance and conquest of temptation. The more we resist, the holier we are. Paul wrote: "We have not an high priest which cannot be touched with the feeling of our infirmities; but was in all points tempted like as we are, yet without sin. Let us therefore come boldly unto the throne of grace, that we may obtain mercy, and find grace to help in time of need." (Heb. 4:15-16.)

Think about the implications of that remarkable statement. The reality of Christ's temptations is the very reason we can have confidence, even boldness in approaching God for mercy, help, and grace in the midst of our temptations. Because he conquered his own temptations, he knows how to help us conquer.

"For in that he himself hath suffered being tempted, he is able to succor them that are tempted." (Heb. 2:18.)

"Behold, and hearken, O ye elders of my church, saith the Lord your God, even Jesus Christ, your advocate, who knoweth the weakness of man and how to succor them who are tempted." (D&C 62:1.)

When the Lord taught his disciples how to pray, one of the things he prescribed was the need to pray for divine assistance in overcoming temptations. The Savior prayed, "Suffer us not to be led into temptation, but deliver us from evil." (JST Matt. 6:13.)

This does not mean that we should pray for deliverance only in the quiet safety of morning and evening prayers. It means that we should cry for help and deliverance right in the heat of the battle, right at the point where we find part of ourselves wavering and considering the possibility of giving in, just as Jesus was tempted at Gethsemane.

In the Pearl of Great Price, Moses recorded a great example of our need to pray *during* our battle with temptation. His battle with Satan came following a face-to-face conversation with God: "He saw God face to face, and he talked with him, and the glory of God was upon Moses; therefore Moses could endure his presence." (Moses 1:2.)

Even though Moses had been "transfigured," the stress of this vision was so exhausting that as soon as the Lord departed and Moses "was left unto himself, he fell unto the earth. And it came to pass that it was the space of many hours before Moses did again receive his natural strength like unto man." (Moses 1:9-10.)

When Moses regained his strength, he realized that it was the Holy Spirit that had quickened or transfigured him so that his mortal body could endure God's presence. This realization set the stage for the battle with Satan. As Moses pondered the marvelous vision, he said to himself: "Now mine own eyes have beheld God; but not my natural, but my spiritual eyes, for my natural eyes could not have beheld; for I should have withered and died in his presence; but his glory was upon me; and I beheld his face, for I was transfigured before him." (Moses 1:11.)

As soon as Moses had realized this, Satan came tempting him. Trying to imitate the glory of God, which Moses had just beheld, Satan appeared to him as an angel of light, saying, "Moses, son of man, worship me." (Moses 1:12; see also 2 Cor. 11:14; 2 Ne. 9:9.) The contrast between God's glory and Satan's artificial imitation was so obvious that Moses was not deceived: "Moses looked upon Satan and said: Who art thou? For behold, I am a son of God, in the similitude of his Only Begotten; and where is thy glory, that I should worship thee? For behold, I could not look upon God, except his glory should come upon me, and I were strengthened before him. But I can look upon thee in the natural man. Is it not so, surely?" (Moses 1:13-14.)

"Where is thy glory, for it is darkness unto me," challenged Moses. "And I can judge between thee and God . . . *Get thee hence*, Satan; deceive me not." (Moses 1:15-16; emphasis added.) Moses had commanded Satan to leave, but he did not leave. For the second time, Moses commanded Satan to depart. "I will not cease to call upon God," he declared, "for his glory has been upon me, wherefore I can judge between him and thee. *Depart hence, Satan.*" (Moses 1:18; emphasis added.)

Again Satan refused to leave. Because Satan hates to lose, he is very persistent. Rarely will he surrender to our first denials. Rather than leave, he offers new inducements and increases the intensity of the temptation. So, instead of leaving, as Moses had twice commanded, Satan persisted, trying to overpower Moses with confusion. "Satan cried with a loud voice . . . and commanded, saying: I am the Only Begotten, worship me." (Moses 1:19.)

This must have been an awesome display of Satan's power, for "Moses began to fear exceedingly; and as he began to fear, he saw the bitterness of hell." (Moses 1:20.) Many of us have experienced similar confusion and fear as we say no to temptation, only to have it increase in intensity until part of us wants to give in and we fear our weakness. It is at this pivot-point of desire that we must obey the Lord's command to pray for deliverance. And it is at this crucial pivot-point that we must not condemn ourselves for being vulnerable.

Twice Moses had resisted. Twice Satan had refused to leave. Yes, Moses was afraid, but he did not allow that fear to isolate or turn him away from God. Instead, like Jesus in the garden, he prayed for additional strength to resist: "Moses began to fear exceedingly; and as he began to fear, he saw the bitterness of hell. Nevertheless, *calling upon God, he received strength,* and he commanded, saying: Depart from me, Satan, for this one God only will I worship, which is the God of glory." (Moses 1:20; emphasis added.)

Still Satan refused to leave! And many times, perhaps even most times, prayer will not immediately remove our temptations, but God has promised that when we focus our faith upon

Christ, we will always be given the strength to resist: "God is faithful, who will not suffer you to be tempted above that [which] ye are able [to withstand]; but will with the temptation also make a way to escape, that ye may be able to bear it." (1 Cor. 10:13.)

Three times Moses had resisted. Three times Satan seemed victorious. Having called upon God, Moses had been given strength, but it had been insufficient for victory. Even though "Satan began to tremble, and the earth shook," Satan did not leave. Again Moses prayed, and receiving additional strength he called upon God, saying: "In the name of the Only Begotten, depart hence, Satan." (Moses 1:21.)

"And it came to pass that Satan cried with a loud voice, with weeping, and wailing, and gnashing of teeth; and he departed hence, even from the presence of Moses, that he beheld him not." (Moses 1:22.)

If a prophet as great as Moses had to persevere and resist temptation four times before finding victory, then surely we should not be discouraged or self-condemning because of our own struggles.

The Lord has said: *"Pray always,* that you may come off conqueror; yea, that you may conquer Satan, and that you may escape the hands of the servants of Satan that do uphold his work." (D&C 10:5; see also D&C 93:49.)

The record of Moses' battle and the Savior's struggle in Gethsemane are not recorded merely for history's sake, but to teach us that *we all need the help of God* to conquer Satan and his Goliaths of temptation. We should never hesitate to ask for divine assistance. As Alma taught: "Withstand every temptation of the devil, with [your] faith on the Lord Jesus Christ." (Alma 37:33.)

THE GOLIATH
OF ADVERSITY

When we accepted Heavenly Father's plan for a mortal probation on earth, we agreed to his condition that there must be "an opposition in all things" we experienced. (2 Ne. 2:11.) Some of our opposition comes through unwanted circumstances we call adversity, trials, tribulations, and suffering. These difficulties are either planned or allowed by God to test and prove us, and to provide experiences that will develop the divine nature within us.

"I will try the faith of my people," said the Lord, "for I have decreed in my heart . . . that *I will prove you in all things,* whether you will abide in my covenant, even unto death, that you may be found worthy." (3 Ne. 26:11; D&C 98:14; emphasis added.) "My people must be tried in all things," he warned, "that they may be prepared to receive the glory that I have for them, even the glory of Zion; *and he that will not bear chastisement is not worthy of my kingdom.*" (D&C 136:31; emphasis added.)

"Prove yourselves unto me that ye are faithful in all things whatsoever I command you, that I may bless you, and crown you with honor, immortality, and eternal life." (D&C 124:55.)

As Brigham Young said, "Every trial and experience you have passed through is necessary for your salvation." (*My Errand from the Lord,* 1976-77 Melchizedek Priesthood Manual [Salt Lake City: The Church of Jesus Christ of Latter-day Saints, 1976], p. 228.)

I was once privileged to help a man who was struggling to overcome sexual perversions and addictions that had controlled his life for many years. (I have permission to share his experience.) Like Butterfly, he had given up hope of ever becoming clean and free of the evils that held him enslaved. And, like Butterfly, his captivity was the result of misunderstanding God's willingness to help us conquer our Goliaths. Like me, he had been trying for years to overcome his Goliath with willpower alone, and each failure had driven him deeper into despair and hopelessness.

As we visited each week, I taught him about the grace of God, which "is sufficient" to overcome any Goliath, and of the Lord's willingness to fight our battles with us in divine partnership. Each week his faith grew stronger, and at last he found real hope of achieving victory.

Then tragedy struck. His wife filed for divorce. After patiently supporting him through thirteen painful years of transgression, her pain was finally so great that she could no longer endure his presence in the home and insisted that he leave.

This forced my friend to decide whether he was trying to change his life because he wanted to be right with himself and God, or only to appease his wife. He decided that if he really could become free and clean through the power of Christ to change his nature, then he would pay whatever price was required, with or without her support.

About six weeks after she had asked him to leave the home, his young son had a birthday. My friend went to the house that evening with a gift, hoping to be allowed to participate in the celebration. His wife informed him that they had already celebrated the birthday the day before as part of family night.

"How could you do that without telling me?" he asked. "Surely you must have known I would want to be a part of it."

Answering from years of accumulated pain, this woman replied cruelly, "We don't plan our life around you anymore."

I can understand the pain that made her say such a thing

and why my repentant friend was cut to the quick. I also understand how eager and skilled Satan is to enter such a situation, to magnify it and to fill our hearts with bitterness, hatred, and revenge.

I feared this incident would so undermine my friend's newly found faith that he would abandon his battle with Goliath and return to his life of sin. I had no idea what I could say that would ease his pain and give him the courage to continue forward with his repentance. But suddenly I heard words coming out of my mouth that I would never have dared to say on my own.

"That's wonderful," I said. "I know it must have hurt you deeply, but I'm glad she said that to you."

He was stunned. So was I.

Silently and desperately I prayed, "Father, I don't understand. Why was it wonderful? Why did you put those words in my mouth?"

The Lord gave me an answer that became, for my friend and me, a sacred learning experience.

"It is wonderful," I heard myself say, "because you now have a tiny taste of the pain and rejection Jesus Christ suffered. And because you have glimpsed this small portion of his infinite sorrow, you can have a bond of fellowship that will draw you to him with a special love and devotion."

Together we realized that no matter how great an injustice or pain might be inflicted upon us, there is nothing we can possibly tell Christ about suffering, about loneliness, about being misrepresented, misunderstood, unappreciated, or forsaken. There is nothing we can teach him about injustice, ridicule, rejection, or about being unwanted, unloved, or betrayed.

The growth my friend achieved after this turning point led him to such spiritual strength that his wife fell in love with him all over again, canceled the divorce, and welcomed him back into her life. Together we rejoiced in God's infinite power to conquer every sin and heal even the deepest of wounds.

Like this man, as we encounter adversity and opposition, we may respond with positive emotions such as trust, submissiveness, and patience, which bring a closer relationship with the Lord. Or we can respond with negative emotions like doubt and resentment, which are typified by the question "Why is God doing this to me?" President Marion G. Romney once said: "I have seen the remorse and despair in the lives of men who, in the hour of trial, have cursed God and died spiritually. And I have seen people rise to great heights from what seemed to be unbearable burdens. Finally, I have sought the Lord in my own extremities and learned for myself that my soul has made its greatest growth as I have been driven to my knees by adversity and affliction." (*He That Receiveth My Servants Receiveth Me,* 1979-80 Melchizedek Priesthood manual [Salt Lake City: The Church of Jesus Christ of Latter-day Saints], pp. 24-25.)

Every Goliath of adversity that we encounter is not only necessary to our probation, but is also promised to work for our benefit. Lehi said that the Lord "shall consecrate thine afflictions for thy gain." (2 Ne. 2:2.) This principle was confirmed when the Lord promised, "All things wherewith you have been afflicted shall work together for your good." During the unjust sufferings the Prophet Joseph Smith endured in Liberty jail, the Lord told him, "All these things shall give thee experience, and shall be for thy good." (D&C 98:3; D&C 122:7; see also D&C 90:24; Rom. 8:28.) Adversity does not happen *to* us. It happens *for* us.

The Lord also said: "He that is faithful in tribulation, the reward of the same is greater in the kingdom of heaven. Ye cannot behold with your natural eyes, for the present time, the design of your God concerning those things which shall come hereafter, and the glory which shall follow after much tribulation. For after much tribulation come the blessings. Wherefore the day cometh that ye shall be crowned with much glory; the hour is not yet, but is nigh at hand." (D&C 58:2-4.)

Similarly, he noted, "These things remain to overcome through patience, *that such may receive a more exceeding and eternal weight of glory,* otherwise, a greater condemnation." (D&C 63:66; emphasis added.)

For God to "work all things together for our good," we must first accept our Goliaths of adversity with patient, willing, and submissive hearts. But God expects even more than a submissive attitude, for as Paul said, we must also be "giving thanks always *for all things.*" (Eph. 5:20; emphasis added.)

It is not easy to express gratitude for adversity. Many times I have to pray, "Heavenly Father, I don't like this situation. It hurts and I don't understand it, but I thank thee for it. I'm asking thee to help me find the good in it, as the scriptures promise. Please show me why I need this. What are you trying to teach me?" He does not always answer that prayer as quickly or directly as I would like. I think that sometimes he withholds the answer because it is more important for me to learn trust and patience than it is to overcome the difficult circumstance. As he told Joseph Smith: "He who receiveth all things with thankfulness shall be made glorious; and the things of this earth shall be added unto him, even an hundred fold, yea, more." (D&C 78:19.)

The principle we must keep in mind when we feel impatient with our adversity is that God has promised to "order all things for your good, as fast *as ye are able to receive them.*" (D&C 111:11; emphasis added.) How foolish and arrogant it is for us to stamp our feet and throw a spiritual tantrum when his will dictates a slower process of growth than we want.

Becoming a "new creature in Christ" is not easy, nor is it instantaneous. Receiving the "new birth" or "mighty change" in our hearts and sinful natures is not an event but a process of growth. Just as mortal birth requires months of preparation and is delivered through the suffering of great labor pains, so it is with the spiritual rebirth. If we would receive the new heart and nature that Christ is working to give us, then we must be willing to bear the pains of adversity with trust and patience, without resentment, complaint, or doubt.

Job set the standard when he said, "Though he slay me, yet will I trust in him." (Job 13:15.)

The Savior told Joseph Smith, "Be patient in afflictions, for thou shalt have many; but endure them, for, lo, I am with thee, even unto the end of thy days." (D&C 24:8.) "And again, be patient in tribulation until I come; and, behold, I come quickly, and my reward is with me." (D&C 54:10.)

Elder Neal A. Maxwell defined patience as "a willingness . . . to watch the unfolding purposes of God with a sense of wonder and awe—rather than pacing up and down within the cell of our circumstance." (*Ensign*, October 1980, pp. 28-29.) Thus, we must be willing to do what is right and to bear our burdens with gratitude and without complaint, "for the people of the Lord are they who wait for him." (2 Ne. 6:13.) Patience with the seeming injustices, trials, and sorrows of life is possible when we look upon them with an eternal perspective, instead of judging them by the immediate inconvenience and discomfort they cause. Recognizing the trials endured by others helps us to bear our own adversity with patience. For example, would I exchange my adversity for a life without the adversity but having been born in Russia? Or Ethiopia, China, or India? Would I trade my adversity for a life in the dark ages? Never. No matter what problems we face, there is always someone who has suffered more. Surely this is one of the reasons the Lord has counseled that we can endure our trials better, and suffer less doubt and frustration in the process, if we will train ourselves to "let the solemnities of eternity rest upon [our] minds." (D&C 43:34.)

The Lord has never promised to remove all our sorrows in this life, but he has promised to be a part of them as he helps us carry the burden. When I feel overwhelmed by adversity, I need only let him know that I need reinforcement, and he always comes through with the extra strength and encouragement I need to keep going. As with all other Goliaths, the Lord is anxious to be a part of our battle with the Goliaths of adversity. "God is our refuge and strength, *a very present help in trouble*." (Ps. 46:1.)

"The way of the Lord is [to give] strength to the upright." (Prov. 10:29.)

"The Lord will give strength unto his people." (Ps. 29:11.)

"He giveth power to the faint; and to them that have no might he increaseth strength." (Isa. 40:29.)

THE GOLIATH OF UNRESOLVED GUILT

True feelings of guilt are a gift of God. The guilty feelings we experience after sinning are given to us by a loving Heavenly Father. This gift of "godly sorrow" is given to convict us of our error, to make us uncomfortable with the sin, and to move us to repentance so that we may return to him. (See 2 Cor. 7:9-10.)

Yet of all the Goliaths that I have seen destroy lives, the lingering and unresolved guilt that haunts so many of us even after our repentance is one of the worst. Sometimes the weight of this guilt presses upon us so heavily that we despair of ever escaping the burden.

I know people who have gone through great sorrow and remorse for their mistakes — people who have paid the price with many years of repentance and obedience. Yet even after being forgiven by the Lord and the Church, even after rebaptism, they continue to suffer unnecessary, useless guilt. This Goliath-sized preoccupation with past mistakes locks guilt in and forgiveness out! We think we are being crushed by the demands of justice, but it is only our failure to take advantage of the atonement.

Often, the greatest barrier to people coming back into the Church is not the continuation of the sins that led to their excommunication, but their inability to forgive themselves and believe God's forgiveness.

Indeed, of all the questions asked of bishops and stake presidents, the most frequent is probably, "How can I tell when I'm forgiven? How can I be *sure* Heavenly Father has really forgiven me?"

If we cannot *feel* the Lord's forgiveness once we have repented and put our lives back in harmony with the commandments, it is not because the Lord has withheld his forgiveness, but simply because it is blocked by the overwhelming presence of our stubborn self-condemnation. Let us explore why it is so hard to feel forgiven; why our feelings of guilt are not resolved and removed after we have conquered our sin and applied all the steps of full repentance.

Jesus left his throne of glory to suffer and die so that *everyone* could have a new life; so that *every person* has an opportunity to start over. But when we decide we are not worthy of his sacrifice and try to make up for that feeling of unworthiness by clinging to our guilt and self-punishment, we lock him out of our hearts and reject the forgiveness he suffered and died to make possible. With Ezra, we are led to cry: "O my God, I am ashamed and blush to lift up my face to thee, my God: for [my] iniquities are increased over [my] head, and [my] trespass is grown up unto the heavens." (Ezra 9:6.)

By slightly twisting and distorting our feelings of remorse, Satan redirects our course away from God so that we find ourselves prisoners, held hostage by his diabolical distortion that *the more guilty we feel, the more repentant and holy we are!* In other words, without realizing what we are doing to ourselves, when we take our focus off the vicarious payment that Christ made for us at Gethsemane and Calvary, and focus instead on our feelings of self-condemnation, we are actually clinging to our guilt and trying to substitute it for the sacrifice Christ already made. In effect, we are saying to God: "Look at me, Heavenly Father. See how angry I am with myself over my weaknesses and sins. Do you see how miserable I am making myself to please you?"

What an awful distortion and tragedy.

We can tell if our guilt feelings are healthy or harmful by

remembering that *true guilt* moves us to repentance and pulls us back to God, while *false guilt,* the distorted, overemphasized, and self-condemning guilt, pulls us downward and builds barriers between us and God.

Guilt alone, without faith and trust in the Savior's forgiveness and atonement, will never bring a change of heart or nature, no matter how sincere the remorse is. Punishing ourselves for our weaknesses, bad habits, and sins does not lift us above them but actually immobilizes and traps us in a vicious cycle of repetition as we continue to act out and reinforce the negative concept we have of ourselves. There comes a time, then, when guilt has done its job and we must let go of it or we cannot move forward.

To let go of our guilt, we must first exercise faith in the Lord's willingness, indeed, his *eagerness* to forgive and cleanse us of our past mistakes. "Thou art a God," said Nehemiah, who is *"ready to pardon,* gracious and merciful, slow to anger, and of great kindness." (Neh. 9:17; emphasis added.) The Lord is never stingy with his forgiveness of the repentant one. Not only is he "ready to pardon," but that pardon is generous and "freely given." "Whosoever . . . shall believe in my name," he said, "him will I *freely forgive.*" (Mosiah 26:22; emphasis added.)

This "freely given" mercy and forgiveness means that the penalty and punishment we rightly deserve is lessened, so that "God exacteth of thee less than thine iniquity deserveth." (Job 11:6.) "Some of you are guilty before me," said the Lord, "but I will be merciful unto your weakness." (D&C 38:14.)

President J. Reuben Clark said: "I feel that [the Savior] will give that punishment which is *the very least* that our transgression will justify . . . [and] . . . I believe that when it comes to making the rewards for our good conduct, he will give us *the maximum* that is possible to give." (*Ensign,* November 1980, p. 31; emphasis added.)

The Lord said: "As oft as they repented and sought forgiveness, with real intent, they were forgiven." (Moro. 6:8.)

"Yea, and as often as my people repent will I forgive them their trespasses against me." (Mosiah 26:30.)

"I, the Lord, forgive sins, and am merciful unto those who confess their sins with humble hearts." (D&C 61:2.)

The very reason Jesus came to rescue mankind was to make forgiveness possible. "This is the gospel, the glad tidings, which the voice out of the heavens bore record unto us," said Joseph Smith, "that he came into the world, even Jesus, to be crucified for the world, and to bear the sins of the world, and to sanctify the world, and to cleanse it from all unrighteousness." (D&C 76:40-41.)

The power of such a statement comes in the personalizing of it. Merely reading the words is meaningless until we put ourselves into the promise. "Jesus came into the world, to be crucified for *me* (whatever your name is), and to bear *my* sins, and to sanctify *me*, and to cleanse *me* from all unrighteousness."

How totally our lives are changed when we realize that he who had every right to judge and condemn chose instead to give mercy and proved it by paying the price of our forgiveness through his own suffering.

"If we confess our sins, he is faithful and just to forgive us our sins, and to cleanse us from all unrighteousness." (1 Jn. 1:9.)

"Who is a God like unto thee, that pardoneth iniquity, and passeth by the transgression of the remnant of his heritage? he retaineth not his anger for ever, because he delighteth in mercy." (Micah 7:18.)

So often we think of forgiveness in terms of months and even years of pleading. But all that time is not required to persuade God to forgive as much as it is to build our faith and to open our hearts to feel and receive the forgiveness he already granted upon our repentance.

Elder Hugh W. Pinnock said, "The Lord forgives us in a millionth of a millisecond." But when his statement was challenged, he said, "Well, perhaps I made a mistake: the Savior forgives us instantly. It doesn't even take him a millionth of a millisecond." (*BYU Devotional Speeches of the Year* [Provo, Utah: Brigham Young University Press, 1979], p. 120.)

So how do we tell when we are forgiven? The way to tell is easy. It is simply to believe God's promise. When he said, "Behold, he who has repented of his sins, the same *is* forgiven," he did not say that we *might* be forgiven, nor that we *could* be forgiven, but that we *are* forgiven. (D&C 58:42.) His forgiveness is automatic: when we confess, repent, and obey, he forgives.

But not everyone is willing to believe that God will do what he said. Sometimes we feel so ashamed of the mistakes we've made that we actually transfer that shame to the forgiveness itself. Without realizing the terrible mistake we are making, we become ashamed of having needed forgiveness, as if it somehow made us inferior. Such feelings are inappropriate, for "blessed is he whose transgression is forgiven, whose sin is covered." (Ps. 32:1; see also Rom. 4:7-8.)

To give assurance that one who is forgiven transgression is just as worthwhile as the person who needed no forgiveness, Elder Vaughn J. Featherstone said: "I have listened to possibly a thousand major transgressions; and each time after a truly repentant transgressor has left my office, I have either knelt behind the desk or bowed my head in prayer and said, 'Lord, forgive him or her, I pray thee. If not, blot my name also out of thy book. I do not want to be where they aren't, for they are some of the most Christlike people I have ever met.' " ("Forgive Them, I Pray Thee," *Ensign,* November 1980, p. 31.)

Our Heavenly Father is not in the business of condemning his children. "God sent not his Son into the world to *condemn* the world; but that the world, through him might be saved." (John 3:17; emphasis added.) To personalize it: "God sent not his Son into the world to condemn me (whatever your name is); but that I, through him might be saved."

Yet, when people struggle with a major transgression, they can really feel condemned by the scriptures. Because I did not understand the Savior's atonement as the solution to my Goliath of guilt, some of the verses I found only increased my hopelessness. For example:

"I the Lord, cannot look upon sin with the least degree of allowance." (D&C 1:31.)

"Do ye suppose that ye can get rid of the justice of an offended God, who hath been trampled under feet of men, that thereby salvation might come?" (3 Ne. 28:35.)

"Do ye suppose that ye shall dwell with him under a consciousness of your guilt?" (Morm. 9:3.)

"I say unto you, can ye think of being saved when you have yielded yourselves to become subjects to the devil?" (Alma 5:20.)

Assuming that these verses condemned *me*, the sinner, I became so hopeless that I was blind to the overwhelming number of references to God's mercy and forgiveness. I came to look upon these kinds of verses as condemning me as a person. But they do not condemn the *sinner*, they only condemn the *sin*. "There is therefore now *no condemnation* to them which are in Christ Jesus." (Rom. 8:1; emphasis added.)

"Verily I say unto you, notwithstanding their sins, my bowels are filled with compassion towards them. I will not utterly cast them off; and in the day of wrath I will remember mercy." (D&C 101:9.)

"For their heart was not right with him, neither were they stedfast in his covenant. But he, being full of compassion, forgave their iniquity, and destroyed them not: yea, many a time turned he his anger away, and did not stir up all his wrath. For he remembered that they were but flesh." (Ps. 78:37-39.)

"For he knoweth our frame; he remembereth that we are dust." (Ps. 103:14.)

After I came to an understanding of the atonement and developed a personal relationship with my Savior, I searched the concordances for every reference in the four volumes of scripture that used the words "justice" and "punishment." I found 297 references. Then I looked up every reference using the words "mercy" and "forgiveness." I found 637! What a testimony to the Lord's infinite compassion and patience with the sinner.

I once heard an interview on the radio in which a man

mentioned that he had four sons, two of whom were adopted. He claimed that he could never remember which two. When I heard that, I thought to myself, that's ridiculous. No one could be so pure in their love as to forget which ones were adopted. No way!

Immediately, the Spirit came into my mind and whispered: "No, Steve, you are wrong. Not only is this possible, it is also an example of what God has said and you have doubted — that when God forgives, he also forgets and remembers the sin no more. You have questioned how a God who knows everything could really forget your sin."

That was true. I had puzzled over that.

And then there came into my mind the impression of a scene. It seemed as if I was standing by the gates to a celestial city as throngs of people entered it. They were so beautiful, dressed in radiant white with indescribable joy radiating from their faces.

I realized that Heavenly Father and Mother were also there with Jesus, watching them enter. I didn't see them, but I could sense their presence and hear what they said. It seemed as if I heard the Savior say to Father and Mother, "Isn't it marvelous to think that some of these people were once so rebellious and filthy that we actually had to excommunicate them from our Church? And now, here they are in beauty and perfection, and they will be with us forever and ever."

And then our Heavenly Mother turned to him and asked, "Jesus, which ones?"

I heard the Savior reply, "I don't remember."

There are many scriptures that support this concept. For example: "Behold, he who has repented of his sins, the same is forgiven, *and I, the Lord, remember them no more.*" (D&C 58:42; emphasis added.)

"I, even I, am he that blotteth out thy transgressions for mine own sake, *and will not remember thy sins.*" (Isa. 43:25, emphasis added; see also Ezek. 18:21-22.)

Once we have confessed and repented, we do not need permission from any person to find our peace and know that we are forgiven. It is a personal experience between the individual and the Savior. There is an important example of this in the Book of Mormon. Enos was alone in the wilderness, hunting and thinking. As he pondered his life, he found much that troubled him. He said that he felt empty and that his soul hungered for comfort. He was so troubled by these feelings that he prayed to the Lord for forgiveness and peace: "My soul hungered; and I kneeled down before my Maker, and I cried unto him in mighty prayer and supplication for mine own soul." (Enos 1:4.)

Nothing happened. He prayed again and again throughout the day and into the night, and still there was no response. We've all had that feeling that our prayers are not being heard. And then Satan whispers that God is not there, or that he is too busy for our petty needs, or that he doesn't care about us because we are so unworthy. What a liar he is. Perhaps sometimes God deliberately delays the answer to our prayers because he knows the more we plead, the more humble and fervent we become, the sweeter our joy will be when the heavens do open to us.

Enos was determined. He decided there would be no peace in heaven until God granted him peace in his heart. Some people are troubled by that kind of persistence, but our prayers do not bother God. What does bother him is when we don't trust him enough to ask and ask until the response is given. Asking is an expression of faith!

When Enos had paid the price, there came a voice from heaven saying, "Enos, thy sins are forgiven thee, and thou shalt be blessed." (Enos 1:5.) Then Enos said something that is crucial to overcoming the Goliaths of our own guilt. He said, "I, Enos, knew that God could not lie; wherefore, *my guilt was swept away.*" Suddenly it was gone! (Enos 1:6; emphasis added.)

Enos was so astonished at the change that took place in his heart that he asked, "Lord, how is it done?" (Enos 1:7.)

The answer he received applies to every person living on

this earth: *"Because of thy faith in Christ."* (Enos 1:8; emphasis added.)

Conquering our own Goliath of guilt is just that simple. Let us consider another example. On their mission to the Lamanites, the four sons of Mosiah brought people into the Church by the thousand. But these converts also faced the Goliath of unresolved guilt. Before they learned about the gospel, they had robbed, raped, and murdered their Nephite brethren and sisters. They had a tremendous problem believing that God's forgiveness was even possible after all that cruelty. However, once they understood and *accepted* the atonement as it applied to *their* sins, they were freed from their feelings of guilt in the same way as Enos. One of them testified: "I also thank my God, yea, my great God, that he hath granted unto us that we might repent of these things, and also that he hath forgiven us of those our many sins and murders which we have committed, *and [hath] taken away the guilt from our hearts, through the merits of his Son."* (Alma 24:10; emphasis added.)

"And if ye believe on his name ye will repent of all your sins, that thereby ye may have a remission of them *through his merits."* (Hel. 14:13, emphasis added; see also Alma 12:33-34.)

Many people are confused and puzzled by the mystery that veils the mechanics of the atonement. *How* does his sacrifice remove the guilt? How wonderful it is that we do not have to understand how it works to receive the blessing. We have only to put our faith and trust in the promise. But there are clues.

Amulek stated that "the intent of this last sacrifice, [is] to bring about the bowels of mercy, which overpowereth justice, *and bringeth about means* unto men that they may have faith unto repentance. And thus mercy can satisfy the demands of justice, and encircles them in the arms of safety, while he that exercises no faith unto repentance is exposed to the whole law of the demands of justice." (Alma 34:15-16.)

It is helpful to identify what "means" are "brought about." Only mercy and Christlike love has the power to lift us. The unthinkable love manifested by the atonement brings about "the means" to change our self-image and feelings of self-worth; to help us see ourselves as God sees us. It provides "the means" to break the stubborn pride of our self-sufficiency; the "means" to set us free from our distorted sense of justice which causes us to cling to our guilt far past the time of repentance; the "means" of giving birth within us of a desire to respond to the great love demonstrated at Calvary and Gethsemane.

We find another clue to the workings of the atonement in 2 Corinthians 5:19, where Paul said that "God was in Christ, reconciling the world unto himself, *not imputing their trespasses unto them.*" (Emphasis added.) If the sins are not imputed to *us,* then what happens to them? Where do they go? What happens to the prescribed punishment? It was laid squarely on the back of our elder brother, Jesus Christ, who already stood before justice as our substitute and paid the price for our forgiveness.

"Thou hast in love to my soul delivered it from the pit of corruption: for *thou hast cast all my sins behind thy back.*" (Isa. 38:17; emphasis added.)

"For behold, I, God, have suffered these things for all, that they might not suffer if they would repent; but if they would not repent they must suffer even as I." (D&C 19:16-17.)

The choice is ours. We can accept Christ's payment and thereby release our guilt and self-condemnation to the atonement, or we can cling to it in misery and waste our probation, never discovering what Eve described as "the joy of our redemption." (Moses 5:11.)

Jack Weyland's novel *Charly* illustrates this principle. It tells of a rather sophisticated nonmember girl from the East who moved to Salt Lake City, where she was converted to the gospel by Sam, a traditional returned missionary who baptized her and eventually asked her to marry him.

After her temple recommend interview with the bishop, Charly told Sam that there had been moral transgressions in her past. Sam couldn't deal with that. The resulting narrative went something like this:

"Charly, did you tell the bishop and stake president about it?"

"I told them everything."

"And they still gave you a recommend?"

"Sam, it was before I even heard about the Church — in New York."

"Why didn't you tell me about this sooner?"

"When I was baptized, you told me my past sins were completely forgiven. Doesn't it make any difference to you that since I've been baptized I've kept the commandments?"

Sam shouted back at her one of the cruelest things a person could possibly say: "I don't want used merchandise!"

He went to see the bishop and told him that he couldn't marry Charly because of what happened before she joined the Church. The bishop didn't understand the problem since she had completely repented.

Sam told the bishop, "She's not clean in my eyes, and she never will be."

The bishop tried to review some of the scriptures on forgiveness, but Sam said, "I don't care about that. You never should've given her that recommend. She's not pure the way I want my wife to be. She's not worthy."

The bishop asked to see Sam's recommend and then locked it in his desk.

"Hey," Sam protested, "why did you take *my* recommend away?"

"Because you don't believe in the atonement of the Savior! Until you do — until you can accept that people can make mistakes and repent and receive forgiveness — you'll never get a recommend from me."

"Bishop, you had no right to take my recommend away, I answered all the questions right."

"Listen, Sam, I'm the bishop of this ward and a judge in Israel. And I say that she's more worthy than you are. Don't you call unclean what the Lord has pronounced clean!" (Jack Weyland, *Charly* [Salt Lake City: Deseret Book Company, 1980], pp. 48-50.)

Isaiah wrote: "Come now, and let us reason together, saith the Lord: though your sins be as scarlet, they shall be as white as snow; thought they be red like crimson, they shall be as wool." (Isa. 1:18.)

And the Lord said: "They shall be purified, *even as I am pure.*" (D&C 35:21; emphasis added.)

An excommunicated woman wrote to me about the resolution of her guilt. Although she had long since repented and been rebaptized, she just couldn't find the peace she longed for and deserved. She said, "I prayed constantly for relief, but the relief didn't come, and I wondered how I could continue life with this weight. What was I going to do? I was totally overcome with sorrow."

Then, after she learned about the personal application of the atonement to her sins, she said: "Finally, one night I left my house so that my sobs wouldn't wake my children. I ran through the cold, dark, windy night, pleading for relief. I couldn't bear this guilt anymore. Surely he would help me.

"Exhausted, I returned to my porch, and while sitting there in despair, I felt my Savior's embrace, the warmth of his bosom, the full essence of the forgiveness and love that he had for me. The pain and anguish floated from my body and has never once returned in seven years.

"Truly his forgiveness does cause us to forget and forsake, just as the scriptures tell us: 'Behold, your sins are forgiven you; you are clean before me; therefore, lift up your heads and rejoice.' (D&C 110:5.)"

THE GOLIATH
OF INDECISION

Two ceramic tiles on our shower wall were slightly loose. For over six months I procrastinated putting new putty in the seam to reseal them. I am sorry I delayed. When I finally got around to the repair, I discovered that my neglect had allowed the moisture to get behind those tiles and rot the wall away. A patch-up job that should have taken only ten minutes cost me over fifteen hours of repair.

The longer we delay making a choice, the greater the heartache and effort it will take to repair the neglect. We gain nothing by delaying our decision to repair the cracks in our life, but we may lose much. *Procrastination is equivalent to spiritual suicide!*

How does your life today compare with a year ago? How will it compare a year from now? What you will someday be, you are becoming right now. Every day counts. Every moment, every decision counts for eternity.

The Lord has provided alternatives to every Goliath. You have the tools and the knowledge to claim victory. If you do not change the direction of your spiritual path, you will end up exactly where you are heading. When the moment of decision arrives, the hour of preparation is past. Every day we must ask ourselves, "If not now, when?" We must remind ourselves continually that "later" usually means never.

It is a sad thing to discover that we are caught in the

bondage of sin, but it is far worse to discover that this is what we want! We laugh at the foolish monkey who puts his hand through the hole to get the banana and then becomes trapped because he won't let go. But how many of us have been trapped by Satan because we won't let go of our favorite sin?

Why not decide to apply the atonement that has already been provided for us? Why not decide right now to invite Christ into our life in a new and powerful way? If we slipped and broke our arm, we would be at the hospital having it fixed within minutes. When we slip and break one of the commandments, we must not compound the problem by leaving it dangling, unresolved.

When we try to ignore or hide our sins, they contaminate us like a spiritual cancer, rotting and festering inside, spreading poison throughout our entire being and pulling us down into the darkness of spiritual death. President Spencer W. Kimball warned: "The longer repentance is pushed into the background, the more exquisite will be the punishment when it finally comes. . . . If men would only let their sins trouble them early, when the sins are small and few, how much anguish would be saved them!" (*The Miracle of Forgiveness* [Salt Lake City: Bookcraft, 1969], pp. 141-42.)

As Christians, we do not repent so that God will forgive us and atone for our sins. The fact that Christ has *already* atoned and paid for our sins prompts us to repent and justify his faith in us. It is because of his unconditional love, offered even while we are in our sins, that we want to respond and bring to fulfillment the forgiveness and changes that he *initiated* in Gethsemane, but that cannot be fulfilled without our participation.

"It is not repentance per se that saves man. It is the blood of Jesus Christ that saves him. Repentance, however, *is the condition required so* that the atonement can be applied in his behalf.

"If one could save himself by a sincere and honest change of behavior, then it could be said that he saves himself by his own works, and the scriptures clearly teach that such is not the case. As Nephi wrote, 'We know that it is by grace that we are saved, after all we can do.' [2 Nephi 25:23.]" (*Doctrine and Covenants Student Manual*, Religion 324-325 [Salt Lake City: The Church of Jesus Christ of Latter-day Saints, 1981], p. 385; emphasis added.)

I have a sister who made her own clothes during her teenage years. Unfortunately, she chose to make the skirts extremely short. One day as she was ironing a skirt, I noticed that it had an enormous hem. I asked her why she had made the hem so large. She replied, "Oh, that's so I won't have to make new clothes when I decide to repent." That is not the kind of commitment to repentance that will lead us to the celestial kingdom.

As a teenager working summers on a farm, I was sent on an errand in the farmer's new pickup. While trying to see how fast I could go, I made a sharp turn on a dirt road, and the back of the pickup slid sideways, almost sending me into a ditch. I stopped the pickup with my heart pounding. Fearful that my recklessness might be discovered, I got out and brushed away the skid marks! We will never conquer our Goliaths and live worthy of the celestial kingdom when we are more concerned about "covering our tracks" than we are about removing the sin.

"Repentance, to be worthy of its name, must comprise something more than a mere self-acknowledgment of error; it does not consist in lamentations and wordy confessions, but in the heartfelt recognition of guilt, which carries with it a horror for sin and a resolute determination to make amends for the past and to do better in the future." (James E. Talmage, *The Articles of Faith*, 12th ed. (Salt Lake City: The Church of Jesus Christ of Latter-day Saints, 1924), p. 112.)

In other words, we must learn to hate the sinning as much as we hate the sin. Perhaps more. Traditionally, we have thought of repentance as the process of "stopping" the sin. But it is always easier "to do" something than it is to "not do" something. When we repent by putting our effort on the positive things we need "to do" to bring us closer to the Lord, we change repentance into a positive process of "going" and "doing." By making the spiritual pursuit of Jesus Christ the focus of our repentance, we will be given the strength to "not do" the things that kept us from him.

I was once asked to give a talk on "repenting and starting over." I don't believe that we can start over. There is no way to undo the sin and go back to the beginning. We can only start from where we are now. That is the place that *every* person must start. No matter what lies in our past, our future is still spotless, and we can choose to keep it that way.

A poor man saved his money for years until he was finally able to purchase passage on an ocean liner. Because the ticket took all his money, he had no means to buy food on the trip. He stayed in his cabin the entire journey, existing on some cheese and crackers he had brought with him.

When the ship finally docked, one of the stewards noticed the man in the line of passengers leaving for the dock. In surprise, the steward said, "I remember you boarding, but where have you been? Why haven't we seen you during the trip?"

Bowing his head in embarrassment, the man confessed his poverty and explained that he had no money with which to purchase meals during the voyage.

"But sir," the steward exclaimed, "your meals were already included in the price of your ticket."

What a waste! How foolish and unnecessary his weeks of suffering were. And so it is with us. We waste our lives living on spiritual crumbs, trying to make it on our own, when we have available to us the infinite riches of the grace and power of Jesus Christ to take us back to our heavenly home.

Let us recognize the unresolved sins we have ignored or hidden and resolve to do whatever it takes to be reconciled with the Lord.

WHO TOUCHED ME?

On the northwestern shore of the Sea of Galilee was a large city called Capernaum. Some of the Lord's greatest miracles and sermons were given in this city, and something happened there that is of profound importance in understanding the Lord's love for us. (See Matthew 9; Mark 5; Luke 8.)

One day, while Jesus was teaching the people along the shore of the sea, the assembly was interrupted by a visitor of great importance. It was Jairus, one of the rulers of the Jewish synagogue there in Capernaum. Jairus had come to plead for the Savior's help in healing his only daughter, a child of twelve who lay in bed, only moments from death. Unable with all his wealth to find a physician who could heal the girl, Jairus cast aside all pride and status and threw himself at Jesus' feet, worshipping him and begging him to heal his daughter.

Because the rulers of the synagogues often led the ridicule and opposition to the Savior's mission, this was a missionary opportunity of tremendous implications. Jesus agreed to interrupt his teaching, and they left immediately on this urgent errand. They were followed by the crowd of people, who were eager to see a miracle, eager to be near the Lord. In fact, so many people were in the crowd, each one trying to be close to the Lord, that it must have been difficult for him even to walk.

In this crowd was a woman with a terrible Goliath, a woman we could say represents each of us. She also wanted to be near the Savior, to look into his face, to feel of his love. But this she could not do, because, according to Jewish law, she was unclean. For twelve years she had suffered a flow of blood, an almost constant hemorrhage.

The woman's sickness was terrible, but perhaps even worse than the physical weakness and suffering caused by this plague was the public scorn it brought her. Judged unfit for marriage, unfit to mingle with the community, unfit to worship in the temple, she was regarded as an outcast, worthless and unclean.

During those twelve long years of illness, she had spent all her money going from one physician to another, always hoping that the next one would have a cure. But none of them had an answer. The scripture says that she suffered many things at the hands of the doctors, things that were sometimes worse, perhaps, than the illness itself.

For all her money and humiliation, her plague had only grown worse. And now, after twelve long, lonely years, there was only one hope left, and that was Jesus.

She believed that if she could only touch the hem of his robe, she would be healed. But unlike the blind or the crippled who called so boldly for his help, she dared not ask. She was not even supposed to be out in public. She was unclean, unfit. And she was separated from Jesus by a crowd of clean people.

Many people have felt that way; that they aren't good enough to be with the Lord; that they have no right to ask for his help; that surely he would want only the clean, moral, righteous people around him; that they are forever separated by what the others are and they are not.

There is good news for people with such feelings, because that is exactly the kind of people the Lord specializes in. Jesus often assured us that he came not to call the righteous but the sinners. He frequently said that the reason he came was to seek and to save those who were lost, those who needed his help.

This woman was free to receive his love because she knew that she had no more defenses, no more substitutes, no more hope but him. It is to that point that we each must come, and when we do we are ready for the message of this woman's experience.

You know the story. She did manage to push her way through the crowd, probably with her face covered so as not to be recognized, and when she touched his robe she felt the flow of blood stop. Immediately she knew that she was healed.

But then, to her horror and the amazement of the disciples, Jesus, who was rushing to heal the dying daughter of Jairus, suddenly stopped and asked one of the most interesting questions in all of scripture: "Who touched me?"

The apostles were incredulous. They asked, "Master, with all these people shoving and pushing, how can you ask 'Who touched me?' "

As his eyes searched the crowd for her, he explained that this touch was different; that it was a touch of faith; that he had actually felt virtue or power flow from his body.

"Who touched me?"

There are other ways to ask that question:

Who trusted in my power?

Who believed in me?

Who applied their faith and made claim upon the blessings I am so anxious to share with each of my brothers and sisters?

Who touched me?

This simple question teaches us volumes about the Lord, about who he is and what he is like.

It shows, for example, that *nothing* escapes his notice.

It demonstrates that no act of faith goes unnoticed, that no petition for help will be ignored. No matter where he is, no matter what he is doing, he will *never* miss the petition of one in need.

It tells us that he can be pressed in a crowd, he can be occupied with important matters, like saving the life of a dying child and influencing the stubborn and blind Jewish leaders — and yet know in an instant when he has been touched by one in need.

It shows that it is the poor and needy, the hurting and hopeless, that come first on his list of priorities.

It demonstrates that it is okay to interrupt God. Our prayers do not "bother him" when we plead for help.

"Who touched me?"

The movement stopped. The crowd was silent.

All eyes turned to the woman, who came in fear and trembling and fell at the feet of the Savior to confess why she had touched him.

For one terrible moment, she must have felt that the whole world had stopped, and her rejoicing must have turned to fear. What if the Lord was angry with her? What if he would rebuke her boldness? What if he took her healing away?

"Who touched me?"

Why would Christ stop and ask that question?

His custom was to tell those he healed not to publicize the miracle. So why did he want to expose this woman to the crowd? He knew who she was. He knew that she was already healed. He knew how urgent it was to help this Jewish ruler who had opened such an important missionary door.

Why delay him?

Why bother the woman?

Why make her confess?

Why not let her go her way in peace?

Or could she?

"Who touched me?" What a divine act of kindness is wrapped up in that question.

To begin with, by asking the woman to come forward, Jesus was able to eliminate any doubt or guilt she may have felt about receiving the healing deceptively. He said to her, "Daughter, be of good comfort." Of even greater value than the healing would be the assurance that he granted the healing willingly, knowingly. "Who touched me?" was a way to put his stamp of approval upon her faith. It was a way of showing her and the public that she was acceptable and worthy of his notice.

A second way this question showed his kindness was by giving her confirmation that her faith was valid. There was no magic in his robe. "Thy faith hath made thee whole," he said.

Third, by asking "Who touched me?" he was able to remove any doubt that the healing was permanent. "Go in peace and be whole of thy plague," he said.

The fourth reason is that it removed from her the burden of proof. It would now be public knowledge that she was clean.

And I think the fifth and most important part of this kindness was the healing of her lonely and aching spirit. What a treasure to remember for the rest of her life that he knew her; he noticed her; he accepted her.

There is a similar act of kindness in the Book of Mormon. It happened when the brother of Jared took the sixteen stones up on the mountain and asked the Lord to use his power to make them shine so that they would have light in their barges and not have to cross the ocean in darkness. (See Ether 3:1-6.)

What happened is significant. One by one the Lord touched the stones with his finger and caused them to shine. He could have done it with a silent command or with a wave of his hand. Instead, he touched them *one by one* because that was a way of saying *sixteen times:* "Yes, my son, you are correct. I do have the power to grant your requests."

Sixteen times he was saying: "Yes, my son, you are right to ask me for help when you have done all that you can."

Each time he touched a stone, he added another assurance of the Lord's desire to be part of our life and to have us walk in the light of his love.

"Who touched me?" What a profound demonstration of the Savior's love and willingness to help us conquer our Goliaths.

PASSING IT ON

Jesus said the duty of all Christians is to love their neighbors as themselves. So, as we learn to conquer our own Goliaths, we should seek opportunities to help others by offering encouragement and sharing with them the power of Jesus Christ to change their lives.

A pilot flew his single-engine plane to a small community where the only place to land was a dirt strip cleared in a field. He arrived over the field just as the sun was setting behind a mountain, and by the time he had circled for a landing, it was too dark to locate the position of the clearing.

There were no lights to mark the landing strip in the darkness, nor was there a control tower or radio to guide him in. To make matters even worse, the plane's landing lights did not work, so there was little chance that the pilot could land without crashing. He was completely helpless. This poor man circled that field for two hours, not knowing what else to do, and knowing that he faced tragedy as soon as he ran out of fuel.

But then a miracle occurred.

Someone on the ground noticed the continuing drone of his engine and realized his predicament. This perceptive man jumped in his car, hurried to the field, and drove up and down the landing strip several times to indicate its boundaries with his headlights. Then he parked at one end so that his car's lights could mark the beginning of the landing strip. The pilot made a safe landing. (Adapted from *Focus on the Family* [Arcadia, Calif.: August 1985], p. 16.)

What an interesting and unusual rescue.

What if someone we know is circling in a dangerous holding pattern, looking for the light to make his or her way to safety? What if God needs us to light the way for someone, and we are not in tune enough to recognize the person's need?

Elder Hugh W. Pinnock told of a young girl who was poor and could not dress like the others. She felt inferior, insecure, unimportant. The students often made fun of her, but there was one boy who would say hello from time to time or give her a "How ya doing?" as they passed in the hall. One day, before they were to take a history test, he saw her in the library and invited her to study with him for a few moments. The weeks passed, and then one day this girl told the young man he had saved her life.

"What do you mean, I saved your life?" he asked in amazement.

"Do you remember the day we had that history test and you invited me to study with you? I was going to take my life that day. I was so tired of having people make fun of the way I dress, of the way I look, the things I say. No one seemed to care. But you cared, and because of that I'm still alive." (*Ensign*, October 1980, p.19.)

I can't help but wonder if there is a person like that in my life. If God needs me to care for someone, will I notice the need in time? Will I reach out and become an instrument in the Lord's hands?

I'm sure you are familiar with Henry Winkler, the fellow who played Fonzie, the "cool cat" with the black leather jacket, on the popular TV show "Happy Days." God even used that character to rescue one of his lost children.

Henry had serious problems accepting that role because he was trained as a classical actor at the Yale Drama School. He had planned to do serious drama, not comedy. He said that even though he looked like a natural in the role of Fonzie, it took every bit of training and skill he had to make that character come alive on the screen. He often wondered if he was wasting his talents, or if the role could somehow do someone some good.

He found the answer to his doubts when he served as chairman of "The Special Arts Festival," held annually in Los Angeles. This event is a kind of Special Olympics of the arts, where children with mental and physical handicaps can go to perform in their own amateur plays, to show their talents and exhibit their artwork.

The children come from all backgrounds and walks of life, and Fonzie loves to walk through the crowds, hugging the kids, holding hands with someone in a wheelchair, joking with a young boy with a missing leg.

Henry's life changed when he heard a tiny, shy voice call out, "Fonzie!" He relates how it seemed strange to him that he even heard the call in the midst of such activity and noise. But somehow, he knew the call had come from a little girl about five years old, with large brown eyes and dark curls.

He made his way over, gave her a hug, and wondered why she wouldn't answer his questions. Supposing she was just shy, he gave her another hug. As he stood to leave, he noticed that the girl's mother had tears in her eyes, but the crowd closed in and he was swept away without a chance to talk to her.

And then one day he received a letter from the mother of the little girl. She explained that her daughter was autistic. (Autistic children are locked in a world of their own and rarely speak or communicate with others. For reasons doctors and psychologists still don't understand, autistic children are so totally self-absorbed that they don't seem to realize that anyone else exists at all.) The mother wrote that her daughter, in the entire five years of her life, had never spoken a single word— until that day she called out, "Fonzie!" Somehow the character of Fonzie had broken through to her, enabling her in that one mysterious moment to make a connection with outside life.

The little girl came to the festival a year later, and Henry eagerly sought her out. This time, her voice was strong and clear as she said: "Hi, Fonzie." As he bent down to embrace her, she pointed at the young girl standing close to them and said, "My sister. Hug her too." In one year she had gained a vocabulary of over fifty words! The doctors were baffled by her progress.

Henry concluded the story with these words: "Sometimes we wonder if we're doing our best for God. We're not sure if we're doing what we should with the gifts He gave us. That little girl showed me that we simply have to do whatever comes our way to the best of our abilities. And then trust that God will find His way to touch someone else with them." (Adapted from *Guideposts,* February 1985.)

What a great testimony of God's power to magnify our efforts as we seek to lift and encourage our brothers and sisters and lead them to a closer walk with God. What if God means for me to be a resource to someone, and I fail to notice? What if I am unprepared? What if someone has to suffer a while longer because I didn't do my part?

Sometimes people resist our efforts to share because they are locked behind those barriers we discussed earlier. They may not even know how to open to us, but God knows, and he will show us if we are ready to listen. Edwin Markham described such a situation:

> He drew a circle that shut me out—
> Heretic, rebel, a thing to flout.
> But Love and I had the wit to win:
> We drew a circle that took him in.

One day an active church member was arrested at a local high school for exposing himself to the students. It was an ugly sin, but he was deeply, sincerely remorseful. He acknowledged his sin to the church. He committed himself to long-range therapy. He even went to the homes of the offended students and apologized. Almost everyone rallied around this brother with forgiveness and support, yet he could not find God's forgiveness because he could not forgive himself.

One Sunday, as the sacrament was being passed, this man left the meeting and almost ran from the building. Could there be any doubt in the minds of the congregation as to how he felt, or why he left?

As disciples of the Master, who said: "I am come to seek and to save that which is lost" (Luke 19:10), what should have been done when this man left? Think how wonderful it would have been if the entire congregation had leaped to their feet and gone after this hurting brother.

Thank goodness one man did. When he got outside the church, he saw that the man was already at the end of the block, literally running down the street. And, bless his heart, he chased after the man and cornered him in a cul-de-sac.

He said, "Please come back. We want you with us."

The man was sobbing, "No! I'm not worthy to be there."

The friend replied: *"Neither are we!"*

Haven't we all sinned and fallen short of the commandments? Aren't we all beggars before God? Not one of us will enter the celestial glory except through the mercy and forgiveness of our Savior. Who are we to judge another?

Jesus suffered such agony for us. And now he asks that we give ourselves in sacrifice and service to each other. I love the beautiful poem that was cited by Corrie Ten Boom in a talk on forgiveness:

> When I enter that beautiful city
> And the saints all around me appear,
> I hope that someone will tell me,
> It was you who invited me here.

EPILOGUE

The Lord knew that we would encounter many difficult situations while working to perfect our characters — situations and obstacles that would often surpass the limitations of our own abilities. But God did not send us here to waste our mortality by surrendering to the Goliaths of this mortal world.

Because of the triumph of Jesus Christ, no sin, no habit, no weakness, no personality or character defect ever need have the last word. We have no reason to waste our lives in misery and defeat. Now that we know the way out of our problems, let us rise up like the children of God that we are, and become the people that Jesus suffered and died for us to become.

Two missionaries in England received a referral to a rather rough part of town. As they left their car to walk to the house, they couldn't help noticing some rather mean-looking characters loitering nearby. When the missionaries came out of the house some time later, these thugs came rushing toward them. The elders ran and jumped into the car and locked the doors. But even though the car was nearly new, it wouldn't start. Not even a click.

The thugs were rocking the small car, about to turn it over!

One missionary prayed for deliverance while the other kept trying to start the car. Suddenly the engine roared to life, and as they drove away, one of the missionaries looked back and wondered why the thugs seemed so surprised.

A few blocks away, they pulled over to thank the Lord for rescuing them. Once again the car wouldn't start.

When they looked under the hood, they discovered that the cables had been cut and the battery removed. (Norma Clark Larsen, *His Everlasting Love*, vol. 2 [Salt Lake City: Horizon Publishers, 1982], pp. 35-36.)

I can almost hear the mechanics of the world saying, "Wait a minute, that's impossible. You can't start a car without a battery." And that's true—unless you have God as a partner.

"Is anything too hard for the Lord?" (Gen. 18:14.) No! "For with God nothing shall be impossible." (Luke 1:37.) The only thing that is impossible is for us to have a problem that is too hard for God to solve. When we find ourselves faced with difficult circumstances or obstacles that seem impossible to resolve, we must ask ourselves where our faith stands: Do I believe that God has the power to help me solve this problem or not? Am I going to listen to Satan or the scriptures?

The brother of Jared said, "I know, O Lord, that thou hast all power, and can do whatsoever thou wilt for the benefit of man." (Ether 3:4.)

The Prophet Joseph Smith said: "Therefore, dearly beloved brethren, let us cheerfully do all things that lie in our power; and then may we stand still, with the utmost assurance, to see the salvation of God, and for his arm to be revealed." (D&C 123:17.)

Whatever your Goliath is, God already has a victory ready and waiting. And you can claim it, beginning now.

Before we part, I'd like you to think about what happened to Peter Cropper, a distinguished British violinist. In 1981 he was given the dream of a lifetime. Because of his contributions to music, the Royal Academy of Music loaned him the use of a Stradivarius violin. This priceless instrument was 258 years old.

In the early 1700s, Antonio Stradivari brought the art of violin-making to its highest pinnacle. Using over eighty different pieces of specially selected pine, boxwood, and ebony, he carefully crafted each violin by hand, and he painted them with thirty different coats of varnish. Stradivari's secret process produced an exquisite resonance that has never been duplicated.

Although he made over a thousand violins, very few of them exist today, and so it truly was the dream of a lifetime for Peter Cropper to have the use of this rare violin for a concert in Finland. But as Peter entered the stage for his performance, the unthinkable happened. He stumbled, fell on the violin, and broke the neck completely off. He was devastated. Borrowing another violin, he somehow managed to complete the performance.

Imagine his heartache as he reported the tragedy to the Royal Academy of Music. They were very understanding and tried to comfort him, but he was heartbroken because of what he had done. Peter could not leave things as they were, and after an exhaustive search he found a craftsman who was willing to attempt a repair.

The repairs were completed a month later. He went to the shop with great trepidation. To his surprise, there was no visible evidence that the violin had ever been damaged, much less broken in half. He couldn't believe it! But the true test would be in the sound. As he drew the bow across the strings, he was amazed to discover that the sound, if anything, was actually more beautiful than before the accident.

Once again Peter took that same violin on tour, and night after night he drew beauty from the Stradivarius that he'd once thought was ruined forever — all because the broken parts were placed in the hands of a master craftsman. (Adapted from an article by Norman Vincent Peale in *Guideposts*, May 1982, p. 42.)

You and I are infinitely more precious than a mere violin. And each of us has the almost impossible task to make it through the concert of life without some damage.

Our adversary, Satan, is working overtime to damage our souls — to break our testimony and destroy our faith. Many of us have already been hurt by him. Some of us feel broken and useless. Some of us struggle with terrible feelings of guilt and shame because of the mistakes we've made. Some of us are held captive by feelings of hopelessness and worthlessness because of the depth of our sins.

Heavenly Father knew that this would happen—as a normal part of our mortal probation. But because of his infinite love for each of us, and because he knew that we could not make our own repairs, he has provided a Master Craftsman for our bruised and broken souls, a Savior who can heal our wounds and repair our broken hearts beyond all evidence of damage.

Will you place yourself in His loving hands?

Will you bring your failures to him and allow him to help conquer your Goliaths?

Will you bring your emptiness and heartache to him and exchange it for the joy of knowing his love and forgiveness?

Even now, he is waiting for you, hoping that you will come.

You may contact the author by writing to:

Steven A. Cramer
P.O. Box 60204
Phoenix, AZ 85082

INDEX